MW00464795

DEAD ON!

Deer Anatomy and Shot Placement
for Bow and Gun Hunters.
Tracking Techniques for Wounded
Whitetails.

John Jeanneney

Teckel Time Inc.
Berne, NY

Dead On!

Deer Anatomy and Shot Placement for Bow and Gun Hunters.
Tracking Techniques for Wounded Whitetails.

by John Jeanneney

Published by
Teckel Time Inc.
Jolanta Jeanneney
1584 Helderberg Trail
Berne, NY 12023
www.born-to-track.com
teckeltime@born-to-track.com

Illustrations by Jolanta Jeanneney and Marilyn Wood

ISBN 978-0-9725089-3-3

Library of Congress Control Number: 2010926948

Disclaimer: Although the author and publisher have made every effort to assure the accuracy and completeness of information contained in this book, we assume no responsibility for misuse or misinterpretation of the procedures and suggestions offered as guidance only.

Acknowledgements

Experienced hunters and some gifted tracking dogs contributed to this book.

The hunters read the book in draft and commented on what they agreed and disagreed with. Many thanks to Kevin Armstrong, Larry Gohlke, Henry Holt, Brian Horl, John Kilroy, Bob Samuel, Don Teddy, Al Wade and Ed Wills.

The dogs could not read the text, of course, but I had "read" them as they worked to show me what wounded deer had actually done far beyond the hunter's point of loss. The tracking dogs who educated me most were Clary, Max and Sabina.

New insights came from across the Atlantic. Philippe Rainaud and Patrice Stoquert showed me the art and science of analyzing the hit site more thoroughly before tracking begins.

My wife Jolanta, the book designer, editor and publisher, showed traits of the predatory hawk as she soared back and forth over the broad expanse of this book's text. Her piercing, merciless eyes could see at once large problems of organization and tiny typographical errors. Big bucks and meadow mice were all fair game. This book would not have happened without Jolanta.

Table of Contents

ABOUT THIS BOOK

For 34 years I have been tracking wounded deer on a volunteer basis. By the end of 2009 I had gone out on 930 searches with my tracking dogs to help hunters. They had tried everything to find their deer before they called me. We found many of these deer, 253 to be exact, and we usually learned something, even if the deer was not seriously wounded, and we could not catch up to it. This book is written to share with you what was learned during these many days and nights in the woods. **You do not need a tracking dog to use this information!**

My earlier book, *Tracking Dogs for Finding Wounded Deer*, describes what the dogs helped me learn about wounded deer behavior. On many occasions the dog's work allowed us to figure out what the wounded deer had done. As the dog followed the scent line, it pointed out the widely separated bits of visual sign far beyond the hunter's point of loss. Most of the deer we did not find provided convincing evidence that they were going to survive. Win or lose, the hunter usually felt better after we were finished. Even if we did not have the venison and the antlers, he knew that the deer was not going to waste.

The tracking dog book has sold beyond my wildest expectations, and many of the readers' comments have echoed these words by Will Elliott: "The abundant wealth of this book lies in what it can do for a hunter before he goes out hunting and wounds a deer. Once a deer has been wounded, Jeanneney's suggestions become priceless for identifying wound sites and tracking approaches before making that call to a Deer Search volunteer handler. Chapters 12-14 alone would be worth the $24.95 price of this book."

This new and smaller book is designed to provide that information, and more, for the majority of deer hunters, who do not have the time or the interest to develop a tracking dog for themselves. They simply need information useful for killing deer quickly, cleanly and humanely, and they need to know the best tactics for finding deer on their own if complications do arise.

As you read this book you will see that my work with tracking dogs taught me many lessons that contradict the traditional lore about finding wounded deer. I had the advantage of learning what happened beyond the hunter's point of loss.

I love to tell and write "deer finding" stories, but too many of these tales can get in the way of presenting clear principles that can be applied in the woods. I want this to be a small book that you can read on the deer stand after 10 AM, once your fingers have warmed up enough to turn the pages. As a former student, and later a teacher, I learned that it is easier to retain information, if you understand why it is true. Without getting into a lot of technical details, I plan to explain the "whys" so that you can remember them, even if your ears are tuned into the forest sounds as you read.

For Those Who Do Not Hunt

This book is written for hunters, but some of those who read it may not be hunters, or may even be anti-hunters. It should be understood that this book does not describe what is typical or routine in deer hunting. The experiences upon which it is based are drawn from 34 years of tracking wounded deer over a region of many New York State counties.

This book deals with the exceptional, unfortunate cases in which deer are wounded and not found. The information is provided in order to help reduce the sad situations described to an absolute minimum. It may seem strange, but sometimes waiting before the tracking begins may actually reduce suffering in the long run.

Those who would use this book as a basis for attacking hunting should realize that an equally disturbing book could be written by an emergency room physician describing about the horrible consequences of automobile travel. In the real world things do go wrong.

Chapter 1

CHOOSING THE SHOT

Doing the right things to get a good shot at a deer is a fine art, and some wonderful books have been written on this subject. This book follows up on these books with advice on actually taking that shot and finding the deer afterward. This information comes into play as you draw back your bowstring or settle your sights on the deer.

Every effort must be made to hunt in such a way that deer will be killed quickly and humanely. Passing up questionable shots is part of being a responsible hunter, but this is not always easy, especially if you are a young hunter or if the deer is a huge buck! However, even with our best intentions something will eventually go wrong. We must be prepared to deal with situations in which the deer was not hit exactly where we intended.

So many unforeseen things can happen. The deer may move unexpectedly. An unnoticed twig or branch may deflect the arrow or bullet. Wind drift may spoil a perfect shot. Then there is the factor of our own excitement! Shooting conditions in the field can be very different from the controlled environment of the shooting range where you sighted in.

This buck took a step forward while the arrow was on the way. The result was a stomach shot.

Should You Take the Shot?

The hunting magazines are filled with good advice about shooting accurately, whether it be with a bow or a firearm. But what is not stressed enough is the big question, "**Is that deer going to cooperate with your intentions?** Is it going to stand still like a 3-D target in an archery tournament?" From other hunters and from my own hunting experiences I have learned that deer are unpredictable in their movements. They take a step forward, they twitch their head and neck, they wheel to the left or right. This is a problem, no matter what arm you hunt with, but the problem is greatest in bow-hunting.

A hunting arrow travels at best 350 feet/second; that would be about 120 yards a second if it maintained a constant velocity. The bowhunter has to consider what the deer might do while the arrow is on the way. Even if the arrow is going to be "on the way" for a third of a second, plenty can happen in the case of a 40 yard bowshot.

In my experience as a tracker, one of the most common cases arising in bow season is arrow placement too far back. As a result the deer has a stomach or intestinal wound. Sometimes I find that these shots are made by superb tournament archers, who can shoot within three inches at 50 yards. They shot with justified confidence that they could hit where they aimed. The problem was that by the time their arrow reached the three inch circle, the deer had moved out of this target zone.

Bowhunting is a different game than 3-D tournaments. **Bowhunting is about the skill of getting close**, close enough, so that the deer has little time to move or react while the arrow is on the way. Personally I like a 30 yard self-imposed limit for whitetail hunting in the Northeast. I know that longer shots are customary in the West. But no matter where you hunt the problem of personal limits for shooting distance must be considered. This book argues that the problem does not have a solution in lighter, faster arrows and flatter trajectories.

The same considerations about shooting distances apply in hunting with a firearm. Of course the speed of the bullet or slug is much faster than an arrow. As a result the problem of the "uncooperative" deer is much less extreme. In most practical firearm situations the reaction time of the hunter, as he squeezes off a shot, is a more important factor than the flight time of the projectile. Still the circumstances in rifle hunting can be very different from shooting at a fixed target. **The answer is to select a target zone large enough to be forgiving if the deer moves.**

When I talk to a hunter who has taken a "head shot", he is likely to say, "I like head shots. It's a clean kill or a clean miss. And I know that I can hit a deer in the head at 200 yards." This hunter may be a fine rifleman, but he doesn't stop to think about how a deer can twitch its head as he tightens on the trigger. The intended brain shot may turn out to be a jaw shot. The deer is doomed to die because it cannot eat, but it may take weeks of suffering before death comes. For days the deer will stay alive, difficult to track and very, very difficult to overtake for another shot. **Head shots are never a good idea.**

Neck shots can drop the deer on the spot, but that narrow zone of the spinal cord and major blood vessels, surrounded by non-vital tissue, also creates an opportunity for things to go wrong if the deer moves. **Avoid neck shots and concentrate on the heart/lung area!**

Shot Placement Basics

The experts all agree that the heart/lung area is the **largest** lethal target area. Yes, you can anchor or kill a deer with shots in other places, but these areas are smaller and harder to hit with certainty. For quick, reliable kills both lungs must be penetrated and collapsed. Then the animal cannot breathe, and it passes out very quickly. Even if hit in this way, a deer can go over 150 yards, and it may give no sign that it has been hit at all.

The heart/lung area is the target zone of choice, but even here the actual dimensions aren't all that over-generous illustrators and deer target designers would have us believe. At best the vital area only begins ⅓ of the way down from the observed topline on the deer. Stylized anatomical drawings and 3D archery targets have mislead us, as hunters, into excessive optimism concerning the placement of "killing" shots.

In the reality of bowhunting, as distinguished from 3D tournaments, the ideal arrow placement on a broadside shot is ⅓ of the way up from the bottom of the deer's chest and **behind** the forelegs. This leaves a safe up and down margin for error. If you see that your arrow passed into the chest above the midline of the deer, prospects are much poorer. Hunters know that the chest cavity begins under the spinal column, but they do not always realize how far this part of the spine lies beneath the apparent topline of the deer. Above the spine itself are the spinous processes, prongs about five inches long that extend upward from the chest (thoracic) vertebrae.

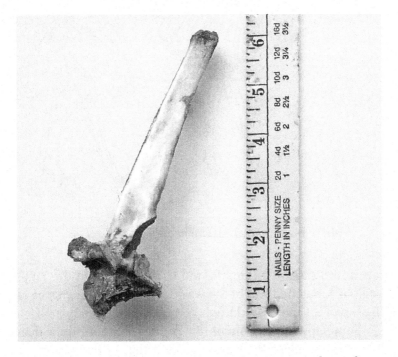

The spinous processes stick up from the vertebrae above the chest. This raises the topline well above the spine and chest cavity.

These prongs angle slightly to the rear, but they add about four inches total height to the deer above the spine. On top of this there is the winter hair along the back. This long, coarse hair pushes the apparent topline even higher above the spine and the chest cavity. When hair and the spinal prongs are

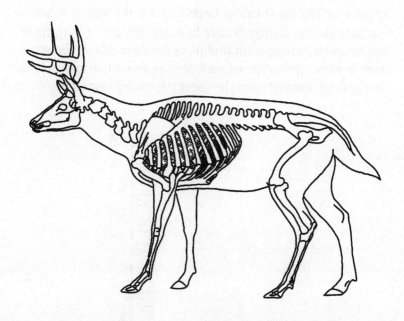

Note that the spine dips down above the forelegs.

taken into consideration, the top of the chest and the lungs begin a good one third of the way down from what we see as the top of the deer. **Hold low!**

Some bowhunters shoot low enough, but lose their deer by aiming to place their arrow within that tipped-backward "V" formed by the shoulder blade and the next bone down, the humerus. The risk of hitting the bones that form this angle is too great. The broadhead may be deflected and fail to penetrate. This happened to me on the first live deer I shot at! **Your aiming point should be three or four inches behind the foreleg and well behind the "V".**

Firearms hunters deal with an enlarged target zone. They may well aim for the midpoint (top to bottom) of the deer's chest, but still any shot that ends up striking higher than the middle third is risky.

Normally a bullet or slug will break the shoulder blade or the humerus below it. However, I have seen two cases, once with a shotgun slug and once with a muzzle loader bullet, where the humerus was broken, absorbing enough energy so that the projectile then skidded around the rib cage behind it and never penetrated. Keep this in mind when taking longer shots with a muzzle loader.

Deflection

The broadside, ground level shot aimed to reach the heart/ lung area is simple enough. The problems arise when we consider how to reach that heart/lung area from other shooting angles. The certainty of reaching the heart/lung area is very dependent upon what you are shooting: bow, shotgun and muzzle loader, or high power rifle.

Arrows, shotgun slugs and muzzle loader bullets are all likely to be deflected by the sloping contours of the rib cage if the projectile does not hit squarely (this is less likely to happen with a high power rifle). **Deflection problems are greatest with head-on shots.** Seen from the front, a deer seems to have a square, blocky chest, not very different in contours from our own. But as you can see from the anatomical diagram on the next page, the shape of the rib cage behind the chest surface is very different. It comes together like the bow of a boat, and there is a small opening in the center. An arrow or a slug, hitting the chest but missing this central hole, will strike the rib cage at a narrow angle. Then it is very likely to slide along the outside of the ribcage, leaving the heart and lungs undamaged. I have tracked deer hit in this way many times. Bleeding is heavy at first, but then it stops and the deer just keeps going.

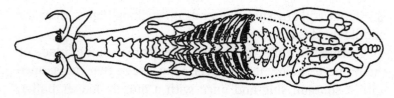

An arrow shot from above can easily be deflected by the sloping ribs of the deer.

Deflection is much less of a problem on quartering shots. Quartering away shots are the best. Think three dimensionally and aim to hit a point above the foreleg on the far side of the deer. Such a shot will always pass through both lungs. If your arrow or slug enters behind the ribs and angles forward through the liver and into the lungs, you will have another very deadly shot.

Avoid Shots from the Rear

Straight, going-away shots kill swiftly only if rifles in the .30-30 class or above are used. An arrow, a shotgun slug or a lighter rifle bullet such as the .243 will probably lose all its energy before it can range forward into the vital area that ensures a quick, humane kill. We owe our game something better than an intentional wound in the butt and the guts.

Special Advice to Bowhunters

We have spoken with hundreds of bowhunters with wounded deer problems stemming from poor shot placement or insufficient penetration. **Keep in mind that there were many *thousands* of other bowhunters who did not have these problems, and did not need to call.** Still it is the goal of this little book to help my fellow hunters prepare for the unexpected times when things do go wrong.

There are many reports of insufficient arrow penetration. If the arrow had continued, it would have killed the deer, but it stopped too soon. Of course blood trails are much better if there is an exit wound. There are several causes for inadequate penetration and the absence of an exit wound.

1. *Arrow was still in flex as it struck the deer.*

Some shots are taken at such close range that the arrow is still fish-tailing. It "slaps" the deer at a slight angle instead of hitting and penetrating head-on. As an arrow leaves the string, it flexes slightly, flexes back the other way and then straightens. The more spine the arrow has, the less flex will be produced and the better the penetration will be. You can test this with your own archery equipment. Shoot into your target at very close range, ten feet or less. You will probably notice that your arrow is sticking out at a slight angle. Move back until you find that your arrows stick into the target at a consistent 90 degree angle. This should be your minimum shooting range in all but low rib cage shots.

2. *An ultra-light arrow and head were used.*

Arrows and heads that are light in weight do produce higher speeds and flatter trajectories. They can produce better accuracy at long, uncertain ranges, but the trade-off is more rapid loss of energy once the arrow enters the deer. Short, steeply angled cutting blades encounter more resistance than longer, more gently tapered, cut-on-contact blades.

3. *The blades were not sharp.*

Blades lose their sharpness over time and through weathering. Resharpen often. Three additional inches of penetration can make all the difference! Two bladed, cut-on-contact heads are most likely to give complete penetration and an exit wound.

4. *Expandable heads were used inappropriately.*

Expandable heads are awesomely effective when they are used appropriately. However, like everything else, expandable heads have limitations, which should be understood. An expandable head is not a good choice if you will be taking shots that require considerable penetration before the vital heart/lung area is reached.

When the expandable heads expand after impact, they begin to lose energy more rapidly than a conventional broadhead of smaller diameter. The blades have to cut a broader swath of tissue, which slows the arrow down. If a bone, such as a shoulder blade or rib is hit, this will affect the speed and depth of penetration even more. I get many calls from tree stand hunters who have a high entry wound and no exit. Often there is insufficient penetration down into the lung area. There will be a few hundred yards of trickle-down blood and then nothing at all. These deer are difficult to track on bare ground. Such shots should not have been taken in the first place. However, the same arrow and expandable head, entering the lower chest at a flatter angle would have produced very satisfactory results.

Expandable heads work best when they are shot with heavy arrows and high poundage bows; they are least effective when they are used with light arrows that lose momentum rapidly after the resistance of the deer is encountered.

Another problem with these "mechanicals" is that almost all cutting ceases once the arrow has stopped moving through the deer. The folding blades then "float" and do not continue to cut back and forth as does a classical broadhead. I probably would not have found the "Columbia County buck" described below if the hunter had used a mechanical broadhead.

Some years ago I took a call in Columbia County, New York. A bowhunter, for whom I had tracked and found deer before, reported that he had shot a deer down into the chest at a steep angle as the buck passed him. There was good penetration, but no exit wound and absolutely no blood. Because I knew the hunter and had confidence in his ability to recognize a killing shot, I took the call.

It was very difficult to get started because many deer had passed later on the same trail taken by the wounded buck. We made several false starts of two hundred yards in one direction before circling back and picking up another line going in the opposite direction. On this one, my dachshund Max seemed more positive, but the trail was obviously difficult. Again, we went about two hundred yards, and suddenly there was a heavy blood trail. Within 50 yards we found the buck dead. Working back and forth with each stride, the broadhead had finally cut its way through the bottom of the chest. By this time the buck's chest had filled up with blood; he had enough power left for only a few more yards before he collapsed. It would have been much more difficult to find this buck if he had been shot with an expandable. It is likely that an expandable would never have penetrated deeply enough to reach the vital area at all.

With experience it becomes apparent that some designs of mechanical heads are much more satisfactory than others. The longest blades do have an especially lethal look about them. However, if you use a head with blades much longer than an inch, you may be creating more problems than you solve. You will be giving up too much penetration.

Heavy bows, heavy arrows and 125 grain conventional broadheads give you the widest range of shot options if your shooting limit is 25 yards.

Steep downward angle shots from a tree stand are often attempted with a bow. They are hard to resist. There is almost no way that you can miss the deer. It may be easy to hit the deer almost directly underneath, but the chances are great that you will never recover it.

First, you have all the problems of hitting the rib cage at an angle, which may deflect the projectile away from the heart/lung area. It is fairly likely that you will get through the rib cage, but then you have a bigger problem. Viewed from above, the lungs of a deer float side by side in its chest like two big sunfish separated by four to six inches. At a steep angle, and a range of 25 feet it is not too difficult to take out one lung, but it is almost impossible to make the double lung shot that ensures a clean kill. I have tracked "one-lungers" for many, many miles. Some ultimately survive; some do not. More on this later.

With an appropriate slug or bullet, steep angle shots, which take out one lung, are much more likely to do the job. Still, with either bow or gun the flat angle shot taken after the deer has passed your tree is more effective.

Special Advice to Firearm Hunters

1. Use Enough Gun

Some people get the notion that it's more "sporting" to use a light deer cartridge. Perhaps they are thinking that deer hunting is like fly fishing for trout. There is nothing sporting about using a light rifle to wound a deer when a .270 would have done the job properly with the same bullet placement.

Gun writers, who churn out hundreds of articles on deer cartridges, are fond of saying that .223s, .243s and similarly chambered rifles are just fine for whitetails provided that there is correct bullet placement. In the real world of hunting, correct bullet placement does not always happen. Why use a light rifle that limits you to a nearly perfect shot? Even if your shooting is excellent, the deer will not always cooperate by standing still.

An adult deer is much tougher than a human of the same weight. Military cartridges like the .223 can put a soldier out of commission, but this does not mean that they will always anchor a whitetail. Too often I hear the same report: "I hit him pretty good, but there was just some hair and a few drops of blood." This generally means a pencil-sized entry hole and no exit, a situation to avoid. If you must use a rifle with a small light bullet, take a flat angle shot through the lower, narrow part of the rib cage.

This is an anecdote, not a piece of scientific evidence, but it so happens that I have had more calls to track wounded deer shot by .243s than calls to track deer shot by all the other deer cartridges combined. Consider using the most powerful firearm that you can shoot comfortably.

The construction of the bullet used is also important. I have tracked for hunters who thought it was OK to use a varmint bullet on whitetails. A bullet that will blow up a groundhog will often blow up on the outside of a whitetail's rib cage. I have seen it happen. Bullets can also be too heavily constructed. A moose bullet may not expand on a small whitetail.

A number of times I have been called to track deer hit broadside in the chest with .308 and 30-06 class cartridges. The deer did not go more than 300 yards, but there was a pencil-sized entrance hole and a pencil-sized exit. Almost no blood. Obviously the bullet did not expand as it was designed to do. I'm in no position to know how common this problem is with rifle hunters as a whole.

I encountered a total lack of bullet expansion myself when I shot a deer at 300 yards with my 30-06. Since the bullet placement was perfect I got the deer, but after that I shot only premium bullets.

2. Always Check Out Your Shot

A beginning hunter sometimes kills a deer with a good heart/lung shot, but loses it due to inexperience. He expects the deer to react visibly and go down immediately. When the deer runs off, apparently unhurt, the hunter assumes that his shot must have missed. Sometimes he does not even go to the supposed hit site to check.

A deer shot with a slug or bullet does not always flinch, stagger or go down suddenly. I have shot deer that showed absolutely no reaction to the hit and yet were down and dead within fifty yards.

Always examine the deer's escape route carefully for at least 100 yards before assuming a miss. Deer sometimes go farther than that before starting to bleed.

It's true that a deer can be knocked down and anchored on the spot with a firearm by aiming higher and farther forward to break both shoulders. Some experts recommend this, but this target is smaller and more things can go wrong if you are slightly off and shoot into the shoulder muscles above the spine. Go for the largest target, which is the high percentage heart/lung area.

With a heart/lung shot you may be compelled to search ahead a bit to find your deer, but this is much better than losing the deer altogether.

Adapting to the Situation

An expert hunter has learned that deer will behave differently depending on the location of the wound. He has developed past the stage of thinking about wounded deer in general. So much depends upon the type of wound and the individual deer. The prospects for survival or death vary enormously. The kind of blood trail the wounded deer leaves will also be a reflection of how it was wounded.

When it comes to choosing tracking tactics for a particular deer, many factors must be considered. Is there a risk that the wounded deer will go on to a private property where you do not have permission to follow? If you cannot get permission, then you have no choice but to hold off on tracking and hope that the deer will die close by. The odds of being able to find the deer vary greatly depending on the wound, the landowner situation and the weather.

Summary

- Concentrate on shooting accurately, but also consider what the game may do just as you shoot.

- Avoid head and neck shots.

- Think three-dimensionally as you select your aiming point on the surface of the deer.

- Aim for the heart/lung area in the chest, which provides the largest margin for error.

- The ideal arrow placement on a broadside shot is $1/3$ of the way up from the bottom of the deer's chest and behind the forelegs.

- Firearm hunters should aim for the middle of the chest behind the forelegs on broadside shots.

- An arrow or a slug can be deflected when it hits ribs at an angle. Know the contours of the rib cage.

- Avoid head-on shots to the chest unless you are using a high power rifle.

• Very light bullets and light arrows lose energy fastest after penetration.

• Heavy arrows and heavy broadheads give the most reliable penetration.

• Sharpness greatly improves arrow penetration. Unused broadheads will not stay sharp indefinitely in your bow quiver.

• Expandable broadheads are risky for steep angle shots that require deep penetration.

• Always check out your shot, even if you think that you missed.

Chapter 2

CHEST SHOTS

Deer Are Tough! When I began my blood tracking career in 1975, it was difficult for me to imagine a deer going very far after an arrow had passed deeply into or through its chest. When, in my lively imagination, I applied such a wounding scenario to myself, I could sense that hemorrhage would be turning out the lights after a few minutes at the most. What has been hammered into me ever since, through many miles of tracking, is that deer are incomparably tougher than human beings. When I began tracking wounded deer, I undoubtedly gave up too soon on certain calls because I underestimated the animal that I had been called to track and find.

This chapter reviews the various types of wounding hits within the deer's chest. One generalization cannot be applied to all of these wounds. In connection with each type of wound, we will review the "sign" or evidence for that sort of wound, the possible behavior and survivability of a deer hit in this way and finally, the best techniques for finding such a deer. This sounds simple, clear and straightforward. Always keep in mind, however, that deer don't read hunting books; they often do what is unexpected or untypical, and a good tracker will keep his mind open to a broad range of possibilities.

Even in bowhunting situations, it is difficult to recall your exact shot placement, and even more difficult to predict the results of the shot. In bowhunting, where the lethal damage is localized to the immediate area severed by the broadhead, a difference of a quarter of an inch, up or down, forward or backward, can create entirely different situations. It can be the difference between a severed major artery and a non-lethal wound that slices a few small blood vessels. Even organ hits cannot be summed up in one simple statement of what will happen and when. For example, two broadheads passing through different parts of a lung can produce either a quick kill or a non-lethal wound. When a beginner gets into this new subject, he should not get hung up on all these fine points and distinctions. The basics must come first, but be aware that things can be complicated and unpredictable. (In firearms hunting the corridor of damaged tissue is much broader; here fine differences in shot placement are not as critical.)

Chest Wounds: Bowhunting

For obvious reasons, trackers do not have to worry very much about heart shots; the heart is an ideal target, but it is also a small target. The practical hunter is more likely to think of the heart/lung area, and, in fact, many more deer will die from shots to the lungs than to the heart.

During bow season, you may need to track a deer that has been hit in the chest with probable penetration of one lung. Such cases will be much more rare for shotgun and rifle hunters. It is possible for a broadhead to pass completely through a lung, narrowly missing major veins and arteries, and not produce a fatal wound. On the other hand, a rifle bullet or shotgun slug does so much more lethal damage when striking the chest in a similar place with a similar wound trajectory. Hydrostatic shock creates a broad corridor of damage.

Hunters, who make chest hits with adequate rifles and slug guns, will usually find their own deer without much tracking effort.

Signs of Chest Wounds

Shots through the heart or the big veins and arteries coming out of the top of the heart do not always produce a great deal of blood on the ground. However, there is generally enough blood for eye tracking, and heart-shot deer never go very far anyway. Two hundred yards is the maximum and almost no heart-shot deer go more than a hundred yards. In over 900 calls, I have been asked to track a heart-shot deer only once. In this case the heart muscle was nicked by the arrow, but the blood-pumping chambers remained intact. The deer seemed to die of "cardiac arrest" as we pursued him about 18 hours after being wounded. We will not have to concern ourselves with heart shots here.

The classic indication of a lung hit is frothy blood on the arrow and in the blood trail. There are many tiny bubbles the size of #9 shot (.08 inch). You may see occasional bubbles in blood from other parts of a deer, but they will be larger (BB size) and not as numerous. After a good shot the successful bowhunter will often see abundant bubbly lung blood on the trail; usually this leads right to the dead deer. Bubbly lung blood does not always appear on the outside. There may be external muscle blood only or even no blood at all. Sometimes the only indication of a lung hit is a round, frothy blood splatter blown from the nostrils.

A pass-through chest shot may seal almost immediately because the deer's chest muscles were stretched as the arrow penetrated. As the muscles slid back across the wound after the shot, they effectively sealed the opening in the chest.

What counts most in deer hunting is internal results. Heavy bleeding on the outside will not tell you whether you have collapsed both lungs on the inside. But you should know that if you make a "double lunger", the deer will be down for keeps within 200 yards. What happens on a one lung shot is more difficult to predict.

Physical Characteristics of Chest Wounds

A review of the chest anatomy of deer is essential if we are to understand the problems that arise in tracking. Note that the heart and the major blood vessels coming out of the heart are located low and to the front of the chest cavity. Blood is pumped from the right side of the heart up into the lungs to be oxygenated; it then flows back into the left side of the heart and then is pumped out through the arteries into every muscle and organ of the deer. Broadheads that slice into this major plumbing at the top of the heart and the front of the lungs kill quickly.

The lower and forward parts of the lungs themselves also have a much heavier concentration of large blood vessels than the portions higher and to the rear. A shot to one or both lungs, low and forward, just behind the forelegs, is going to kill the deer, whether it is a broadhead, a bullet or a shotgun slug that does the job. If only one lung is damaged and the wound is higher and farther back, problems begin for the bowhunter. A broadhead cutting into the pink spongy tissue (alveolar tissue) of the lung, high and to the rear, will slice the microscopic blood vessels or capillaries, and some medium-sized vessels as well, but there may not be enough blood lost, internally or externally, to kill the deer.

The damaged lung will collapse and cease functioning, but this is not too serious if the other lung is intact. Deer, like humans, can function reasonably well on one lung. In addi-

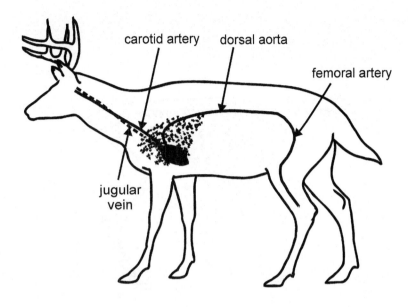

Major blood vessels

tion, the smaller blood vessels in the damaged lung tend to constrict due to lack of oxygen when the lung collapses. Blood flow through this lung is greatly reduced, and therefore, major hemorrhage fails to occur. One lung hits are not necessarily killing shots for the bowhunter. This distinction is less important for firearm hunters because of the greater tissue damage produced by bullets and slugs.

Hunters should always try to take out both lungs in order to collapse them both and make it impossible for the deer to breath. In bowhunting this is not as easy as it sounds because most shots are taken from tree stands with the hunter looking down on the deer. Taking out both lungs together can be difficult or impossible. When shooting downward at a steep angle at a broadside deer, it is easy to shoot over the near side lung and hit the far side lung too high to kill the deer.

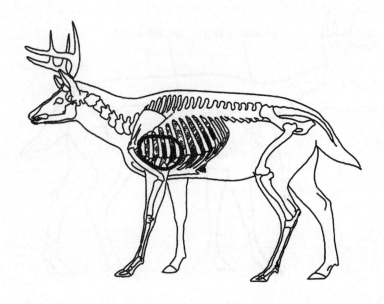

Target zone for bowhunters

When shots are in the chest area, the difference between the work of arrows, on one hand, and bullets and slugs, on the other hand, is most apparent. The arrow does not produce hydrostatic shock like the slug and bullet. If the arrow passes all the way through the chest, and it does not hit anything important enough to bring death within a half hour, then the chances that the animal will survive are quite good. Broadheads cut cleanly and do not pull in hair and other material that might contaminate the wound. The broadhead is not

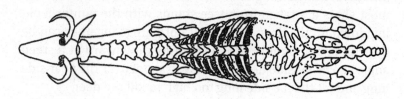

sterile, but the deer's healing (immune) system can generally deal with the small amount of infection that develops. Slugs and bullets, on the other hand, produce a broad zone of damage and may even collapse lungs when they pass nearby. They also carry hair into the wound, which can cause serious infection to the rare deer that does not die quickly.

Every bowhunter education course stresses that frontal shots into the chest should not be taken. Unfortunately, when no other shot presents itself, even experienced bowhunters can forget the lesson. In the previous chapter we discussed how the deer's rib cage draws to a point in front like the bow of a ship. If the arrow does not penetrate almost exactly into the center of the chest, it strikes the ribs at a narrow angle and is deflected to the rear without ever penetrating the chest cavity. It is likely to pass between the rib cage and the shoulder blade or the next bone down (humerus), cutting muscle tissue and producing a heavy blood trail because all of the bleeding is external. The deer will lose serious amounts of blood, but normally the flow slackens before the point of no return is reached. From an archer's eye view, this looks like an excellent chest shot, but this is an illusion. Unless the arrow passes through the small "window" at the front of the chest, it is seldom fatal.

Usually I receive about one call a year that fits this description. They are hard to screen out on the telephone because there is no way of being certain whether the broadhead passed inside or along the outside of the chest. If you cannot blood track the deer beyond a quarter of a mile, your arrow or slug probably passed on the outside. To be certain have a tracking dog check out the line.

In the fall of 2000 I tracked a large buck with a distinctive rack that had been shot from the front. The buck went almost straight up a small but very steep mountain. The hunter was certain that he could not go far with such a massive hemorrhage. The deer lay down after reaching the top, rested and then went on without bleeding. Two weeks later the buck was observed in the same area. He was moving well.

Bow shots to the chest, taken when the deer is quartering toward the hunter, are more effective than head-on shots, but there is still some possibility that the arrow will be deflected along the outside of the rib cage. It is better to let the deer pass by or turn to a more broadside position.

Like the shots taken directly from the front, quartering shots from the rear can be difficult to diagnose with certainty. Try to have your arrow enter behind the rib cage to range forward through both lungs.

Finding Chest-Shot Deer

Deer shot with a sharp broadhead often have little awareness of what has happened. They are in shock, feel weakness and sense that something is wrong. If you see them lie down, the best option is to wait and see if they expire. If they keep moving, they will try to return to a secure place, and this may involve circling back to a place close to where they were shot. In any case, they will try to remain in their home territory or return to it. A rutting buck, roaming out of his territory in search for does, is likely to take off in a straight line for his home turf immediately after being hit.

If you can determine that the arrow entered the deer's chest halfway down from the topline of the deer, the chances are very good that you can find it. Of course, it is best if the arrow went precisely where it was aimed, one third of the way up from the bottom of the deer and right behind the shoulder.

Any shot taken at an angle into the rib cage can be deflected so that it never enters into the vitals of the chest cavity. Shots that angle forward into the chest from an entry point in

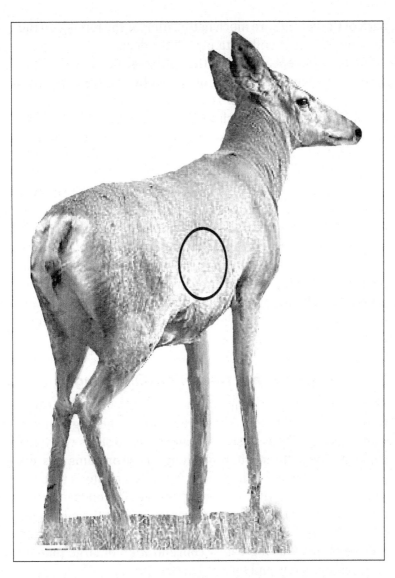

Target zone for bowhunters on mule deer doe quartering away.

back of the ribcage are much better. Aim for the foreleg on the *far* side. This shot will certainly kill the deer.

It's worth repeating that the course of the arrow to the vital heart/lung area can be deflected by the rib cage. This can happen when the deer is shot high in the back at a steep downward angle into the chest. It turns out that there is little blood because there is no exit wound. The arrow remains just beneath the hide and does not come out. Such a shot should never have been taken.

Sometimes the arrow is not deflected but penetration is poor; all but 8 or 10 inches of the arrow are sticking out of the deer as it takes off. Generally, these poor penetrations develop because the shot was taken too close and the arrow was still in flex and fishtailing as it struck the deer. On these poorly penetrating shots there is not much that can be done, especially if the hunter is using expandable broadheads. An experienced tracking dog will be able to check out the deer's trail much farther than it can be eye-tracked.

Survival of Bowshot Deer Hit in One Lung

There is no easy and simple advice to give concerning chest wounds in bow season. Try to reconstruct the angle of the shot as accurately as possible. Many of these shots will have damaged and collapsed only one lung. These one lung hits are never a sure bet, as we have seen, but it is a hunter's responsibility to follow up in every way possible. The odds improve greatly if the arrow entered the deer lower than the midpoint. Generally, the lower and more forward the entry, the better are the chances. The greatest concentration of large pulmonary vessels is low and forward in the lungs.

In cases of chest-shot deer in bow season we have learned that the odds of finding a deer are greatly reduced if the deer travels over a half mile or stays alive for more than a half hour.

This means that your broadhead did not cut any major blood vessels. The small vessels severed will clot up, and the deer will either recover or die much later. But keep trying, even if the chances of success seem slim. There are no certain rules in bowhunting. There is no sure way of knowing whether you severed a minor artery or missed it by a quarter of an inch.

In an unknown percentage of cases bowshot deer do survive wounds to one lung. On one call my dog and I arrived late in the afternoon, about eight hours after the buck had been shot. All the classic signs of a lung hit were present. In the first hundred yards from the point of impact there were drops of blood that still showed fine bubbles no larger than number nine shot (.08 inch). A few of these were even present on the arrow, and smears of blood on the right side of the trail up to a height of 24 inches suggested that the deer had an exit wound about two feet above its hoofs. The hunter confirmed that this must be the exit wound since he had shot the deer from the left side. The blood trail dwindled rapidly to a drop every hundred yards or so, which was the reason that Arnold had called me in the first place. However, it was easy enough for the dog, and we tracked about 600 yards to the deer's bed. We heard the deer depart in the dense undergrowth, and a few drops of blood in the bed confirmed that we had jumped the right deer. To shorten a long story, we pushed this deer "that had to be dead" hard for over two miles. We never got close to it. This buck was observed two weeks later.

This has happened many times since. Often hunters have called back to report seeing the deer again, alive and well a few days later. Hunters have reported a buddy taking the same wounded deer later during the gun season. One bowhunter even shot the same deer he had wounded earlier that fall.

Back in 1977 I was perplexed by these situations in which deer, clearly lung shot, were proving to be unrecoverable. I organized a research team of biologists I knew and they examined 51 deer that were shot in an intensive, one-day bow hunt at the Howland Island Waterfowl Refuge in Cayuga County, New York. Deer were brought to the check station gutted, but with chest cavities intact ahead of the diaphragms. Out of the 51 deer, one doe, a year and seven months old, had clearly survived an arrow wound in one lung while she was a fawn. She was in good health and weighed 101 pounds, normal for her age and the area. The sample size is not large enough to constitute "scientific proof" concerning deer survival, but there is certainly enough anecdotal evidence to justify some serious research.

The theory, still held by some wildlife biologists, that a breach of the vacuum in the chest leads to a fatal collapse of both lungs does not seem to apply in many bowhunting situations.

Remember that not all pass-through shots, reported as lung shots, actually involve the lungs. There is such a thing as being too far forward. I can think of a case a few years back when I tracked a bear, which had been shot the day before low behind the foreleg. In this case what applies to bear applies to deer. The bear had been angling away, and unfortunately, the bowhunter did not think three-dimensionally and adjust his point of aim to the rear. The arrow angled through the very front of the chest, ahead of the heart and lungs, and exited from the brisket on the far side. There was no visible blood except for a few smears on saplings, but there was plenty of scent and the bear was easy to track. He kept going and we never came to a bed or any evidence of hot bear scent.

When you track a chest-shot deer during bow season be aware that it may be difficult to follow because the entry wound is high and there is no exit. The first blood from a high

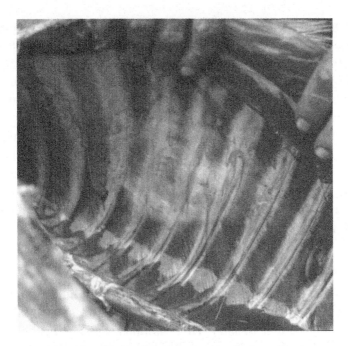

Howland Island doe - scar on chest wall.

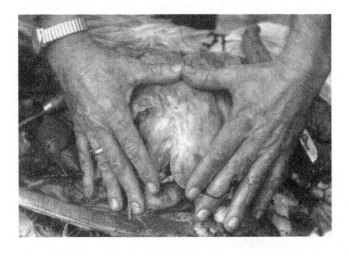

Howland Island doe - scar on lung.

hit may be some distance from where the shot was taken because it takes time for the blood to trickle down off the side of the deer onto the ground. You may be able to verify the line for a while by blood on the ground, but then as bleeding slows, the last traces of blood will probably be on smears above ground level. Be sure to look for them.

It is useful to have some sense of the odds of finding a chest-hit deer. As previously stated, a general rule on chest hits in archery season is that **if the arrow is no longer in the deer, and the deer has been able to live a half hour and travel over a half mile, it has an excellent chance of survival.**

Chest Wounds Made by Firearms

It must be very rare that an appropriate rifle bullet or shotgun slug enters the chest cavity and does not end up killing the deer sooner or later. There is much damage inside, and the external wounds, especially the exit wound, are likely to stay open and disrupt breathing. Usually there will be the same heavy bleeding, and often the same frothy lung blood that is typical in bowshot deer.

One of the biggest problems for the tracker in rifle or gun season involves determining that a valid chest hit is involved. You don't want to spend hours searching for a deer that was merely grazed or perhaps missed altogether. Hunters attempting to find wounded game should think positively, but positive thinking can slip easily into wishful thinking. Every hunter wants to believe that he hit where he aimed, and he usually aimed at the chest. If the bullet actually missed the heart/lung area and did not break the spine, most likely it went high and grazed the back. It is especially easy to shoot high with open sights.

In my experience, many deer are lost because chest hits turn out to be high back shots that are mishandled. Again and again, every year I hear the same story: "I hit him right in the chest, and he dropped like a ton of bricks. I didn't bother to shoot again because he was finished. Then he jumped up and ran off." Deer hit in the chest rarely drop on the spot. They may stagger, stumble, make a few jumps and collapse, but they will not drop instantly unless the central nervous system is temporarily or permanently knocked out. Instant knockdowns are discussed in Chapter 5, which deals with high back wounds.

When assessing the possibilities of a chest shot, the handler should use all that he knows about the alternative situ-

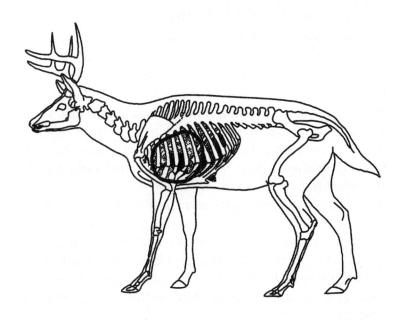

Target zone for firearms

ations that might have occurred. Many head-on "chest shots" turn out to be wounds that break the shoulder blade or the humerus, that heavy leg bone directly beneath the shoulder blade. These leg hit situations are discussed in Chapter 4.

Grazing shots, which do superficial damage, are another possibility, particularly with frontal shots and in the case of quartering away shots when the hunter does not hold far enough back to shoot diagonally through the heart/lung area. Here, one giveaway is a larger than normal quantity of hair that has been raked off by the slug. Another indication of the same thing is hair still attached to flakes of skin, which were scuffed off as the slug plowed along the surface. Detailed analysis of this is presented in Chapter 5.

Indications of Chest Wounds

Deer hunting books often show illustrations of how chest-shot deer react by lunging straight forward. But Richard B. Smith in his excellent book *Tracking Wounded Deer* points out that deer sometimes have no immediate reaction to a lethal chest shot. I have taken lung shots myself, which put the deer down within 25 yards. Yet these deer gave no detectable sign that they had been wounded. They just trotted or ran off. Their tails usually stayed down, if they were already down when the shot was fired.

At other times the reactions of deer do confirm the hunter's hopes that he has made a good shot. Deer that are already spooked and have their tails up are likely to clap their tails down, but there are exceptions to this. Such deer may lunge straight ahead in the best classic form. Other deer stagger visibly, but do not go down until they have run for several hundred yards.

Usually a valid chest shot will produce ample blood on the ground, and you will quickly find your deer. However, in shotgun and rifle hunting it can happen that the high chest shot produces lethal bleeding, which pools in the chest cavity and never spills out on the ground.

It may seem strange that a slug wound does not always bleed from surface tissue at the entry and exit, but I have seen this happen. In one case the torn-up shoulder muscle produced by the exiting 12 gauge slug made a wound too big to cover with my hand, and yet this button buck traveled over half a mile and left only two nickel-sized drops of visible blood and a splatter of bloody foam blown from his nose.

If there is no blood on the outside, even 200 yards can be a long way in heavy cover. A lack of tracking blood may result when a high power rifle bullet fails to expand. Modern high power rifle bullets are generally very reliable, but in my rather limited experience with rifle bullets in chest shot situations there have been at least two cases where .30 caliber rifle bullets did not expand and passed right through leaving pencil-sized entry and exit holes. The weight and design of the bullet used in these two cases seemed to be a reasonable choice for deer-sized game.

As said before, when small caliber, centerfire cartridges such as the .243 and smaller are used, there can be problems. There is a small entry wound and often no exit at all. Most hunters don't have a sufficiently good reason to use small caliber, light bullets.

Summary

• Bowhunters should always aim to take out both lungs. This is impossible when the deer is directly underneath the stand.

• Head-on chest shots offer a small and narrow target.

• Internal bleeding kills many deer that lose little blood externally. Search hard even if you see very little blood.

• Lung blood has many tiny bubbles. A few large bubbles do not assure a lung hit.

• If a chest-hit deer travels more than a half mile, the chances of recovery go down. But keep trying!

Chapter 3

GUT SHOTS

The loose term "gut shot", as used by hunters, is usually applied to the whole area of the animal's body cavity in back of the diaphragm, which separates the heart/lung area from the other organs behind it. The diaphragm is an all-important dividing point between two very different types of wounds that require very different strategies for finding the deer. It's important to realize that part of the main stomach and part of the liver extend well up into the rear portion of the rib cage. These organs are separated from the lungs only by the thin muscle tissue of the diaphragm. 3-D targets often create the false impression that the lung area extends all the way back to the last rib.

When hit in the stomach, liver or intestines, deer are almost always doomed to death although the results are not immediate. Finding the deer is largely a matter of time, patience and not making mistakes. And it does make a big difference where in the "guts" the deer is hit. If you want to get serious, distinctions have to be made between the stomach, the small intestines just behind the stomach, and the large intestines to the rear. The liver and kidneys are smaller vital areas, which never stop bleeding when damaged. You would not choose them as a primary targets, but they are invariably fatal.

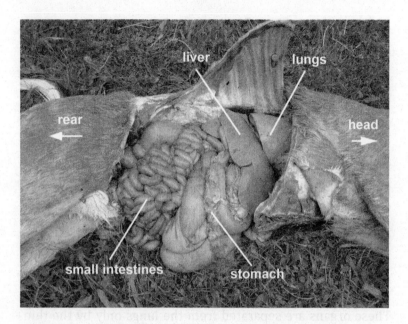

Going from right to left this photo shows right lung and directly behind it the liver, main and small accessory stomachs. The lungs and the digestive organs are separated by the diaphragm, which does not show here. The front of the liver and stomach lie within the rear of the rib cage. The small intestines lie behind the stomach.

Signs of a "Gut Shot"

Gut shots often occur because the deer takes a step as the bullet or arrow speeds toward the chest. Generally the animal hunches up as it is struck.

Deer hit in the stomach or intestines usually bleed very little externally. Certainly the seriousness of the wound can't be judged by the amount of blood that is left on the ground. Most of the bleeding will be internal; this internal bleeding empties the arteries and veins as effectively as external bleeding, and it has the same lethal effect.

Blood from the stomach and intestines is usually dark and muddy looking. It may contain fragments of food, grass, browse, acorns, corn, etc., and it may be quite watery from digestive fluids. If the wound was made by an arrow, and the arrow was recovered, the area it passed through can usually be determined by closely examining the broadhead and fletching and by smelling the arrow. Tiny flecks of food material are usually stuck in the angles of the broadhead and around the base of the fletching. The arrow that has passed through the stomach will also have a distinctive "cow barn" smell. Cows and deer are both ruminants, which eat some of the same food, and have similar types of stomach bacteria breaking it down during the digestion process.

If the arrow passed through farther back, the smell will be more like deer droppings and the smears of material on the arrow will be of finer, darker material.

The blood line that the hunter sees can sometimes be misleading. Most of it may be bright red muscle blood, not the dark blood of a stomach or gut shot. The bright blood actually comes from the outside layers of the deer and not from the digestive organs. It requires only one drop of dark blood among a 100 bright ones to confirm that you are tracking a stomach or gut-shot deer, a deer that will suffer and probably be wasted if you give up too soon.

The lower belly of a deer is covered with coarse, chalk-white hair. If you find this on the ground, it will most likely have blood on it indicating the exit wound of a gut shot. Remember that the inner thighs, the rear and the tail are also white. If you hit farther forward and low in the brisket, the hair will be almost black and slightly kinky. A low brisket shot that does not penetrate the body cavity is not a fatal wound.

Physical Characteristics of Gut Shots

Technically a deer's long stomach system is partitioned into four sections. The first and largest of these is the rumen, where 40% of the nutritional value of the deer's food is absorbed. The other three sections of the stomach and the small intestines also absorb nutrition, but to a lesser degree. These highly absorptive areas of the gastrointestinal tract have the highest density of blood vessels, and a broadhead that does damage here kills most quickly. Within the wall of the rumen itself there are many tree-like branchings of blood vessels. If the main branches are severed, the deer dies quickly, often within half an hour. If the arrow passes between the main branches of blood vessels and cuts only fine capillaries, death may come after 12 or 24 hours or even longer. Likewise, an arrow cutting into the first section of the small intestine, which has many small blood vessels, can kill very quickly.

Veterinarians have observed that in cattle a hole high in the rumen is not necessarily fatal because the contents of the rumen do not drain into the abdominal cavity. The wall of the cow's stomach can heal itself. It is likely that the same thing can happen in a deer that is shot high in the rumen.

An arrow placed farther back, which cuts the large intestine or bowel, has little immediate effect on the strength and viability of the deer. There are fewer blood vessels here as this large gut is mainly a holding place for waste to be excreted.

The worst intestinal hits, from every standpoint, are those that take the deer high in the abdominal cavity beneath the loin. These are called "peritonitis hits" because death comes very slowly from blood poisoning as body wastes seep into the blood supply from the damaged large intestine.

The blood trails from stomach-shot deer have a peculiar characteristic that the hunter should understand; the drops or splatters of blood from the inside of the deer are turned on and off as if by a faucet. What happens is that the perforated stomach rotates as the deer travels along. When the arrow wound in the stomach lines up with the arrow wound through the outside of the deer, dark blood from the stomach spills out onto the ground. When the stomach rotates slightly and the openings move out of alignment, leakage to the outside is sealed off and there is no blood to track. Often, it is at one of the "turn-off points", with no blood to be seen, that the hunter loses the track and can progress no farther. At these times a tracking dog can save the day.

In these cases it does not seem to make much difference to the tracking dog whether there is visible blood or not. At all times there is plenty of scent coming down from the wound. The dog continues tracking with a confidence that the handler should share.

Liver Wounds

The liver is located in front and along side of the stomach directly behind the diaphragm. Usually an arrow piercing the liver will pass through the stomach as well. Pure liver blood is characteristically a dark, almost maroon color.

One of my best learning experiences occurred when I was asked to track a deer that, as it turned out, had been shot in the liver.

A friend had first taken the call with his very promising, but still inexperienced young wirehaired dachshund. Waldie, the young bitch had tracked the deer out of a swamp, across a field, through a passageway in a stone wall and across a road into a cluster of spruce trees next to a house. There the trail seemed to end. The hunter even inquired at the house about whether someone had picked up the deer.

I was invited to give it a try with Clary, who was Waldie's dam and a much more experienced tracker. Clary trailed from the last dark liver blood up to the house, just as her daughter had done. At the dead end she made several small circles and headed back across the road and through the same opening in the stone wall. This time she passed through on the opposite side of the opening and headed down across the field by another route. At the edge of the swamp, I saw one pinhead-sized drop of blood on an alder branch. We tracked over a mile, seeing no more blood, and I sensed growing doubts on the part of the hunter. Clary was positive. Finally we climbed up a long hill and there at the top lay the six-pointer, dead. He had gone to a safe spot where he could observe or smell danger coming from any direction. The slug had passed through the center of the larger lobe of the liver. The buck had not been pushed, but the last thing that he had done was climb a long, steep hill.

Kidney wounds and damage to the renal arteries that supply the kidneys are fairly rare, but the tracker should always remember that they do occur. The kidneys are located under the backbone and just behind the last rib. This is further forward than most hunters realize.

Blood passes through the kidneys via the renal arteries and the renal veins at a rapid rate. A wound here will quickly

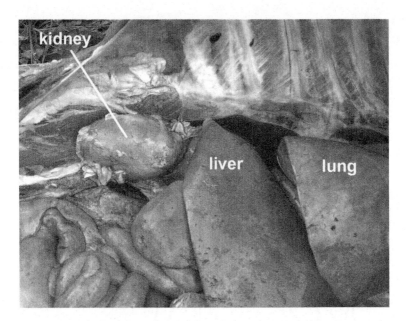

Photo of kidney (fat removed) just below spine and just behind last rib.

result in a lethal loss of blood. There is enough blood volume and pressure in the renal arteries to produce a spray of blood on weeds and brush as the deer passes.

From a hunter's standpoint there is no certain way of predicting the timetable of events after a deer has been wounded in the gastro-intestinal system. But if the deer eventually survives, it is certainly a rare case. The tracker should be very persistent.

Finding Gut-Shot Deer

Almost always the best strategy for the tracker is to wait as long as possible when there are strong indications of a stomach hit. Generally there will be tracking blood at the beginning, but if he follows up too soon, he will bump the deer out of its first bed after it has stopped bleeding externally. He will have no blood trail to work with, and his best recourse will be to call for a tracking dog.

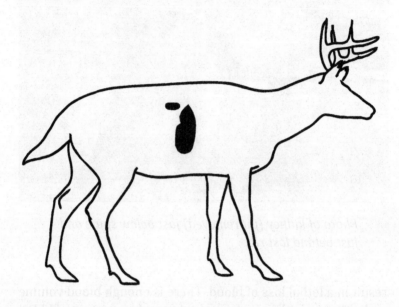

Diagram of the liver, which is located to the rear and side of the main stomach. Farther to the rear are the kidneys, which lie just under the spine behind the last ribs.

Wounds to the intestines behind the stomach create similar problems. In these gut shots the timetable is also influenced by which part of the intestines has been damaged. Wounds to the small intestines that are involved in digestion generally kill as quickly as stomach wounds because there are many small blood vessels there. As we have said above, placement of the shot by the hunter can usually be determined by the behavior of the deer at the shot (hunching), by the scent on the arrow, if it is recovered, and by the special character of the blood sign observed.

Eight hours might be the ideal length of time to wait on stomach and intestine hits. However, almost always there are other factors that must be taken into consideration in deciding when to begin tracking. Is the weather so warm that the deer is likely to spoil if it is already dead? Eight hours in bow season, if the temperature is above seventy, can be too long a time. Are there coyotes in the area? A night's work by a family pack of coyotes will leave very little venison for the hunter. In heavily hunted areas, is there a strong likelihood that someone else will find the deer?

This Illinois buck was shot in the late afternoon and tracked the next morning. The coyotes got there first. Photo by Henry Holt.

Finally there are weather conditions. The eye-tracker has to consider whether rain or snow is predicted. If visible blood is rained out or covered with snow, he may have to resort to a tracking dog. Rain or up to four inches of moist snow are not a problem for a good tracking dog.

Another last resort for finding gut-shot deer is to check ponds, streams and any bodies of water, which are in the area where the deer was lost. Gut-shot deer become dehydrated and feverish. We often find them dead next to the water or in the water where they went for their last drink and to cool off. Water does not seem to have the same degree of attraction for deer with other types of wounds, but if you know that the deer is gut shot, keep water uppermost in your mind. Carefully search all water surfaces for a gray-brown bulge of the deer's side. Deer with their winter coats always float, but the head and hindquarters hang down and most of the deer is not visible.

Summary

• Be alerted to a gut shot by even a small percentage of dark blood. Most of the blood may come from the outside layers of the deer.

• Gut shots are easy to track, but wait at least four hours before beginning.

• Deer sometimes survive chest shots with an arrow, but very few survive gut shots.

• Find your deer before the coyotes eat him.

• Gut-shot deer are likely to go to water.

Chapter 4

LEG AND MUSCLE WOUNDS

When deer are wounded in the fleshy parts of their legs, with no bones broken, they can be expected to recover. They may leave a strong blood trail at the beginning, but there will not be enough blood loss to kill the deer. The muscle tissue will heal. When the leg bones are shattered by a bullet or slug or even by a broadhead, the situation is very different. Such deer may lose the affected leg and heal up as a three-legged deer. However, the long term prospects for such a deer are poor, particularly in areas of heavy snows. Such handicapped deer cannot feed as efficiently, and they have difficulty escaping from predators such as coyotes. There are exceptions, but according to Glenn Cole, who was New York State's Region 3 Wildlife Manager for many years, few three-legged deer with old wounds show up at Highway Check Stations. This suggests that most of them did not survive the winter after they lost their leg. It is better to track down these deer and kill them as humanely as possible, rather than to let them face a lingering death or a very difficult life.

Signs of Leg Wounds

Often a deer whose foreleg is broken will be reported as having been shot in the chest. However, there are a number of signs that clearly indicate that a leg has been broken and can no longer support the deer's weight. After the deer is shot it will often stumble and fall once or twice **when it attempts to run**. After a fall or two the deer departs rapidly on three legs. This is an entirely different case from the **instantaneous** collapse that occurs when the spinal column has been damaged or shocked.

The area around where the deer was struck by the hunter's projectile should be carefully checked. If the bone has been hit, it is almost always possible to find some bone fragments on the ground at the point of impact or in the first few hundred yards of the trail. These fragments may look like "pieces of rib" but they almost always turn out to be from the leg bones. If you are really serious, it is a good idea to collect samples of the major bones and familiarize yourself with their contours. Then in many cases you will be able to match fragments with your sample bones. It took me a long time to realize that the presence of a few leg bone chips does not always mean that the leg was broken.

Generally, the higher on the leg the break occurs, the easier it will be to track and recover the deer. The high break will not freeze up or dry up as rapidly because more muscle tissue and larger blood vessels will be involved. The deer will drag its leg or it will swing back and forth, accelerating the bleeding. On the other hand, if the break is low, beneath the knee or hock, the deer will hold its hoof off the ground. There will be less agitation and less bleeding.

The blood itself will be bright and difficult to distinguish in color from blood flowing out of a flesh wound. However, it will often be distributed in many small droplets, and more reliably, a broken and swinging leg will leave bloody drag marks over branches and logs lying across its trail. In dry, loose leaves there will be drag marks if the wound is high enough so that the deer cannot hold up its foot.

On soft ground or sand another sure indication is that the track made by the hoof opposite the damaged leg will be deeper, and the points will be abnormally spread because of the extra weight carried.

Splayed hoofprint of deer with opposite front leg broken and unable to bear weight.

A deer with a broken leg is likely to leave blood smears like this over branches on the trail.

Physical Characteristics of Leg Wounds

A deer with smashed leg bones will bleed heavily for a quarter or a half mile, and then the bleeding will greatly diminish or stop altogether when the deer halts. Much of this bleeding after the shot comes as a steady dripping from the exposed marrow ends rather than from blood vessels supplying the leg muscles. If the deer can stop, stand and cease its exertions, this blood flow from the marrow will begin to clot up. (There is considerable difference from individual deer to individual deer in how fast this clotting takes place.) Mud packed in the wound or freezing of the end of broken bone will also stop the bleeding in very cold weather. We have seen a few exceptions, but generally the leg below a broken bone loses its blood supply and eventually sloughs off.

Tactics for Recovering Deer with Broken Legs

Absolutely nothing is to be gained from waiting before tracking a deer if you know that the deer is wounded in the legs. The problem is that many hunters, unaware of exactly what has happened, track a short distance and then decide to wait and "let the deer stiffen up", as hunting folklore recommends. Leg hits should be tracked promptly, just the opposite of the long waiting period appropriate for a known gut shot.

There are two advantages to tracking a known leg hit right away:

1.   In the first ten or twenty minutes the deer is likely to be in shock. By tracking with care, watching for the deer all the time, you may be able to get a second shot before shock wears off and the deer collects its wits.

2.   If the deer is allowed to stop, the bleeding is likely to diminish to nothing. Blood clotting, and perhaps freezing, will make continued eye-tracking very difficult when the deer is jumped from its resting place.

For these reasons it is important to determine quickly just how the deer has been hit so that the appropriate tracking tactics can be used. First reconstruct in your mind the behavior of the deer at the shot. A leg-hit deer does not go down instantly in total collapse as is the case in a high back shot. Often it will take a step and then go down as the damaged leg collapses under its weight. The deer may get up and fall down once or twice and then take off on three legs. Sometimes they do not fall at all. Look for a loosely swinging leg.

This deer was tracked two miles before it could be ambushed.

This deer left nickel-sized drops of blood for four miles before it ran out of power.

If you don't have a pretty good idea of where the deer was shot on the basis of after-the-shot behavior, the next step is to go to the hit site. Approach the hit site carefully. Keep looking all around you for the deer as you move. First, mark the hit site and then search carefully for evidence of what happened. You will be looking for hair, blood and of course for leg bone fragments.

Once you understand the situation, get on the blood trail of a deer with a smashed leg as soon as possible after it has been wounded, particularly in very cold weather. Do this before the exposed leg bone dries or becomes frozen. Movement will raise the deer's blood circulation rate higher and maintain the blood flow. The broken leg will swing back and forth, and that will also maintain the bleeding. If the deer bleeds nickel-sized drops every ten feet, you can probably walk the deer down. It may well require four miles or more at a fast pace to accomplish this. If the leg wound does not begin to bleed again, it is best to back off since there is little prospect of tracking fast enough to catch up unless you have snow.

The dog and handler can track far faster than the unaided hunter tracking by eye, and it is this speed that puts pressure on the deer and keeps it bleeding. You may only see a nickel-sized drop every ten feet or so, but more blood is being lost in fine droplets as the broken leg works back and forth. It is an easy track for the dog to follow and rarely is the deer lost because the dog loses the trail.

If large streams or lakes are approached, it is better to ease up and avoid driving the deer to water. Deer learn from being chased by coyotes and free running dogs that water is a final resort of escape.

Before they are a year old, leg-hit deer will sometimes give up after a very short time. A seasoned adult is a very different animal with enormous toughness and stamina. A mature deer, especially a tough old buck, will go full power up and down hill almost until the end. Once the deer allows you to approach within fifty or a hundred yards while it is lying down, the end is very near and not in doubt.

Don't worry if you encounter a sudden disappearance of blood sign in this last stage of tracking. As the deer's blood pressure falls, the bleeding may stop, and this is further evidence that the deer is about to drop. It is common to see no blood at all on the last 200 yards of the trail before coming up on the deer unable to go farther. This is true, not only in cases of leg hits, but also in any sort of tracking situation where the deer is being pushed, has lost large quantities of blood and cannot go much farther. Don't quit when you are on the verge of overtaking the deer!

Blood Sign and Muscle Wounds

Muscle blood is generally bright red, and there will be a lot of it on the ground because all of the bleeding is on the outside. The color and length of hair cut by the broadhead, slug or bullet help to identify the site of the wound on the deer. The placement of smears of blood on weeds and brush are also important. Blood that has spurted out under pressure indicates that an artery has been cut. The odds of finding the deer greatly improve when the larger arteries are involved.

Inexperienced hunters who see dinner plate-sized pools of blood are certain that this guarantees that the deer lies dead somewhere over the next ridge. But such a quantity of blood from the ham of an adult deer guarantees very little in itself. A lot of blood may flow out from the smaller veins and capillaries of a deer's thigh, but if the bleeding stops there will seldom be enough blood loss to kill the deer. Usually you will find that the bleeding from muscle wounds clots up before an adult deer is in serious jeopardy.

The femoral artery is a high volume, high pressure blood pipe that feeds the massive thigh muscles of the deer. It runs through the muscle close behind the femur or thigh bone, hence its name. When the femoral artery is cut, blood loss is so rapid that the deer goes down within 50 yards. The femoral artery should never be an intentional target; it is scarcely more than half an inch in diameter when filled with blood and is a difficult target. The femoral artery can be ruptured by a slug or bullet that plows through adjacent tissue. In bowhunting, a miss of the femoral artery by a mere quarter of an inch produces a muscle wound that is unlikely to produce more than exercise for the hunter who tracks a mature deer.

Tactics for Muscle Wounds

It is very important for the hunter to determine if the deer has been hit exclusively in muscle tissue, or whether the external muscle bleeding is masking more serious bleeding from the deer's internal organs. Generally, you must track an adult deer to a wound bed to determine its condition. A cold bed with little blood suggests that the deer was strong enough to leave voluntarily. If you find that the deer has stopped bleeding, is moving well and jumping fences, you are usually pretty safe in deciding that the deer will survive.

Fawns, young deer that were born the previous spring, are much easier to recover when they have muscle wounds. Sometimes the tracker can walk right up to them, or the fawns quit after moving out a hundred yards from their bed.

Once a deer has lived through a winter and has matured, it becomes a very different animal. Adult deer don't quit. A tough old buck is like a truck; he goes up hill, down hill, wherever he wants to go as long as there is gas in his tank. Only when he is totally out of gas does he collapse, and generally this happens suddenly. A mere muscle wound will not reduce him to this point unless there are special circumstances.

Snow cover can make rapid tracking more feasible. In this case a determined eye-tracker can push a deer faster and harder. This can produce more bleeding, weaken the deer and give opportunity to approach for a shot.

Significance of Blood on the Ground

To sum up the subject of blood sign in muscle hits, the amount of blood is much less significant than the type of blood and its placement. For example, the amount of external bleeding on a muscle-shot deer may appear to be identical to what was seen in another case where the deer was recovered dead after a modest distance. In making comparisons about real blood loss, both internal and external bleeding must be added together. Let's face it, such calculations are impossible for a hunter to do under field conditions. A strong trail of muscle blood on the ground for a few hundred yards does not mean that the deer is bleeding to death.

Particularly when a big buck is involved, it is easy to overestimate the volume of external blood loss. Actually it does not take much blood to make a very good blood trail. In dog training we have discovered that it is easy to lay a visible blood trail for over a half mile with only a half pint of blood. With a full pint (half a quart) you could produce quite a few good-sized pools of blood in the track. Yet a pint of blood is the amount that a deer-sized human loses when donating blood. The drawing of this pint of blood from our own bodies, when we donate at the Blood Bank, has little effect upon us.

I have had a few hunters on the phone report "gallons" of blood on the ground. When I got to the hit site, the amount was much less, of course. For your own estimates it helps to know how much blood is actually in a deer, and how much blood loss must occur before the deer reaches the point of no return. A whitetail weighing 150 pounds on the hoof has about eight pints of blood, that is four quarts or one gallon, in its whole circulatory system. The deer has to lose about 40% of this amount, roughly 3½ pints, before blood pressure falls to a point where irreversible shock sets in. The deer then slips into a coma, and all its vital processes spiral downward. For a 150 pound deer it will take nearly 2 quarts of blood loss to put the deer down. This is a lot of blood.

There is another useful thing to know about the amount of blood to be seen on the trail. When a deer is bleeding to death from internal or external bleeding, or a combination of both, it is easy to lose the blood trail near the end. For the last 200 yards before he goes down for good, there may be no visible blood at all. When visible blood ends, it is not the time to quit! At this point, it is likely that the deer's blood pressure has fallen to the point where there is no external bleeding. He will not go much farther.

Deer in the final stages of collapse due to blood loss are still capable of a final burst of energy. The handler should remain alert and cautious. I can remember an instance when a bowhunter shot a finishing arrow into a buck that we had just caught up to. The buck lay in front of us on a knoll with head flat, eyes closed and legs tucked beneath its body. At the arrow shot, he leaped straight up, and I saw him in the air higher than my head. When he landed the next jump was directly toward me; then he veered away and ran down hill. The buck collapsed again within 50 yards, and that was the end.

Hair at the Hit Site

Most of the white hair on a deer comes from the hindquarters or the lower parts of the deer. The belly hair is very coarse; the long white hair is finer on the inside of the thighs and the hind end. Of course the underside of the tail is white. There is a patch of shorter white hair at the deer's throat. The brown hair of a deer is located on the back and sides, the forelegs and the outside of the thighs and the rear legs. The brisket or sternum, the bottom of the deer's chest, will have dark, rather short hair that is slightly kinky. It is unlike any other hair on the deer.

The brown body hair gives rise to some confusion because the lower two thirds of each "brown" body hair is actually light gray or beige. Sometimes in poor light these hairs are reported to be white. It is generally possible to recognize hairs cut at the entry from those cut as the arrow, slug or bullet exited. Some of the hairs at the exit will be matted with blood or tissue. Putting this information together with the known angle of the shot permits a reconstruction of the trajectory through the deer.

Make up a collection of hair samples like this that is appropriate for your region of the country. This photo shows a hair sample collection produced by Gary Huber of Deer Search Inc.

Since there are many sub-species and variations of whitetails in North America there is no way to give general descriptions of the color and length of hair on each part of a deer's body. The hair patterns vary from sub-species to sub-species. For example, the South Texas whitetail is lighter in color and very different from the whitetail of the Northeast. In addition, hair grows throughout the hunting season. The coat of a deer on October 1 is much shorter than it will be on December 1. If you wish to do a precise analysis of hair sign, the best thing is to make two hair sample booklets for your particular locality, one for the early and one for the late stages of the hunting season.

This photo shows a large quantity of hair resulting from a grazing, high back shot with a 12 gauge slug.

Close-up of top photo showing ½ inch piece of outer skin with hair attached.

The amount of hair found at the hit site can be a valuable indication of how the deer was hit. If you see a fistful of hair, it is a sign that you have raked or grazed the deer. This is often seen on high back shots as well as muscle shots. A slug or bullet hitting squarely will cut some hair but a much smaller amount.

Some of the hair may be attached to a tiny patch of outer skin; this is another sign of a grazing hit. It is worthwhile checking to make sure that the slug did not hit a branch on the way in to the target. Too many hunters fail to inspect the hit site carefully and some do not check it at all because they do not realize its importance.

Summary

• Begin tracking deer with broken legs as soon as possible and keep them moving.

• Muscle shots that stop bleeding seldom kill the deer.

• A fistful of hair at the hit site suggests a grazing shot.

• The color and placement of blood has much more significance than the amount of blood that you see on the ground.

• Fawns quit sooner than adult deer.

Chapter 5

HIGH BACK SHOTS

What could be more certain evidence of a perfect shot than the instant collapse of the deer? **Think again.** Many deer are lost every year by misreading this situation.

We are giving high back shots their own special chapter because these are so important and so misunderstood. High back shots are one of the least understood events in the deer hunting experience. How can a deer be hit so hard that it collapses instantly and yet sometimes runs off to escape? The only good thing is that most of these high hit deer that escape survive to live healthy and wiser lives. Problems with high back hits arise almost always during the gun season. I have encountered a few cases where deer were stunned and knocked down by a direct arrow hit to the spine, but these are rare.

Gun shots to the spinal area fall into two broad categories. If the deer is down with a broken back or damaged spinal cord, all that is required is a well-placed finishing shot in the neck or low in the rib cage behind the foreleg. **A somewhat higher shot above the spine can produce identical immediate symptoms, and yet have a very different result.** After collapsing as if struck by a great hammer, the deer regains consciousness and coordination, stumbles to its feet and is gone, usually forever. The hunter was so confident that he had killed the deer that he became careless. He did not think about taking an insurance shot until it was too late.

I hear variations of this high back shot scenario year after year. If only deer hunters could better share the lessons learned from their experiences!

A hunter called me in the early 1980's and told me a story that was at once funny and sad. It more than sums up all the other tales of woe that we hear each season. The hunter in southeastern New York asked me to come and find his deer. He had shot his buck and thought that he had killed it instantly; it had dropped and did not move. The first thing the hunter did was to take a photo to preserve the moment. He rested his sling-equipped shotgun in the forks of the buck's antlers. As he stepped back with his camera to take the photo the buck shuddered and lurched to its feet. The hunter never found his shotgun and never found his deer.

Signs of a High Back Hit

The most important evidence suggesting a high back shot is the *instant* knockdown. There is no way of knowing immediately whether the spine has actually been broken or whether the deer has simply been stunned. If the deer struggles to its feet and takes off, you will know for sure that its back was not broken!

At the hit site another indication of a high, grazing back shot is a large quantity of hair shaved off by the bullet or slug. The photo on page 67 shows an amount of hair that was actually produced by such a shot. In contrast, a solid hit, striking the deer squarely, produces only a thimble-sized amount of hair.

High blood smears on weeds and brush are another give-away, although the eye-tracker concentrating upon what is on the ground will often miss this. The average buck in New York is only about 34 inches at the shoulder so be concerned if there are smears above 28 inches in height.

Never base all your judgment upon one piece of evidence. I remember tracking and eventually catching up to a deer that showed us one waist-high blood smear near the beginning of the trail. It turned out that the deer was wounded just above

Blood smear on brush at waist level. This deer collapsed instantly at shot. The overconfident hunter was looking for another deer as this one got up and escaped.

the front hoof. The deer was jumping when it left the high smear on a bush!

Physical Characteristics of High Back Hits

What happens in many cases is that the nerves of the spinal cord, running through the spinal vertebrae, receive a massive jolt from the high-energy slug or bullet passing in close proximity. If the projectile hits or passes close to one of the prongs (spinous processes) that stick up from the chest vertebrae, this readily transmits shock to the spinal cord. The deer may stay down a few seconds, a few minutes or forever. However, if it gets back on its feet and regains its coordination, it is generally impossible to catch up to that deer.

Above the spine there is enough muscle tissue to permit considerable bleeding, but ordinarily this bleeding does not continue long enough to kill the deer. With damaged back

Coyotes dissected this buck nicely to show the spinous processes above chest.

muscles the deer may not run well, but it will keep walking without difficulty. Of course, there are exceptions to everything! In the fall of 1996 I tracked a deer that had been shot across the loins above the spine and was very dead. In this very unusual case a mechanical broadhead with wide cantilever cutting blades had produced enough external hemorrhage to kill the deer. The only reason I was called in to track it was because the deer was shot in a snowstorm that obscured the heavy blood trail.

Rifle shots that pass closely *beneath* the spine can produce the same temporary paralysis as an above the spine shot. Here, the large dorsal aorta artery that runs along beneath the spine will probably be ruptured by the same impact. The deer will be dead of blood loss before it can get back on its feet. Deer shot with firearms directly below the spine do not have to be tracked.

If the shot is actually below the dorsal aorta, it will certainly pass through the top of one or both lungs. In a healthy deer there is no "dead space" between the top of the lungs and the top of the chest cavity.

What are reported as high chest shots often do not enter the chest cavity at all and are actually well above the spine. As discussed in Chapter 2, many hunters do not realize that the length of the *spinous processes* and the length of the hair along the deer's top line can make the top of the deer appear to be six inches or more above the actual level of the main mass of the spine.

Arrows shot into the upper ribs may be deflected horizontally into the spine, seldom killing the deer. An arrow shaft, sticking out horizontally from the deer near the topline is an indication that this has happened.

Dealing with High Back Shots

In the woods there is no sure way that you can tell whether you broke the deer's spine or merely shocked the spinal cord. Forget about bragging about a one shot kill! Shoot the deer again in a place that will destroy little venison. If the deer gets away, you will have no venison at all! A low rib cage shot or a well-placed neck shot is good insurance in this case.

If a prompt "insurance" shot is not taken, there is no very productive strategy for dealing with the situation when the deer gets up and takes off. Keep your eye on the deer as you approach!

Summary

• If the deer goes down instantly, be ready to shoot again. There is no way of telling immediately whether the deer has a severed spine or is merely stunned.

• If a deer that went down instantly is allowed to get up and go, it is generally gone for good.

Chapter 6

NECK AND HEAD SHOTS

Neck Shots

The general rule with neck shots is this: **the hunter gets the deer very quickly or he does not get it at all.** The heavy vertebrae of the neck are highly vulnerable to a slug or bullet, but a broadhead, striking in the same place, may or may not get through and sever the spinal cord. Especially for bowhunters the spine is not a good target. Below the spinal column in the neck lie major blood vessels: the branching carotid artery and the jugular vein. If these are severed, there will be a solid six inch path of blood to where the deer collapses. If the spinal cord in the neck is not damaged or if major blood vessels are not cut, a neck wound is unlikely to be fatal, at least for a very long time.

Signs of a Neck Hit

Even on the less serious neck hits (bow and gun) there is usually quite a bit of visible blood. The hunter should be able to track by eye for at least 300 yards. Some of the blood he sees will be high on brush and branches and generally there will be blood spots on both sides of the trail.

Usually there will be little internal bleeding on neck shots. What you have seen on the outside is the sum total of what the deer has lost. Since a deer's neck is narrow, an arrow usually passes completely through. There will be no further damage from an arrowhead working about. Because of this same narrowness of the neck, a bullet or slug will pass through with minimal expansion if no bone is encountered. The wound channel and the shock will normally be less than in a chest hit.

Physical Characteristics of Neck Wounds

As explained above, breaks of the spinal cord and wounds to those big blood vessels, the carotid artery and the jugular vein, are swiftly lethal affairs. Especially when a carotid artery is cut, the brain is starved for blood and oxygen and the deer loses consciousness. Beyond the spinal column and these major blood conduits, there are not many good places to hit a deer in the neck. Of course, a high velocity rifle bullet striking almost anywhere in the neck may still generate enough shock and damage to anchor the deer for a second shot. But a shotgun slug, particularly if it passes through the fleshy area above the vertebrae and ahead of the shoulders, will not accomplish very much. For a bowhunter the situation is even worse. If he misses those narrow lethal targets in the neck, there are no acceptable secondary targets. Cutting the esophagus or food pipe will not kill the deer for a very long time. If his broadhead cuts the trachea or windpipe, he may realize what has happened when he hears whistling and wheezing. Unfortunately, if the deer does die eventually, only the crows and coyotes will be there to enjoy it.

Again, we must go over the exceptions. In bow season if the broadhead has stayed in the deer's neck, the broadhead will work back and forth. Sooner rather than later, it may cut far enough to create a sudden hemorrhage and death to the deer.

Near the top of a deer's neck two tendons hold up the head and neck. If both tendons are severed, the deer is in serious difficulty and cannot hold its head up. It is possible to walk the deer down. This situation rarely occurs.

Most non-lethal neck wounds are simple pass-throughs in the fleshy tissue above the spine. The buck is soon ready to feed and chase does again.

Head Shots, Jaw Shots

There are hunters, particularly riflemen, who prefer head shots. "Clean kill or clean miss," they say. "You don't spoil any meat." A young bowhunter once told me, "I took the head shot because the rest of the deer was behind a tree. It was the only shot I had."

Anyone who has worked very much with wounded deer will condemn head shots under any circumstances. The question is not always one of marksmanship; deer often move their heads quickly and unpredictably as the shot is taken. The result is not necessarily a clean miss; it can mean a smashed jaw and a deer which cannot eat or drink. Any injury that damages a deer's teeth and its ability to browse and chew is a mortal injury for that deer. It will not be a quick clean death, but rather a slow lingering one from starvation.

The deer's brain, which is about the size of your clenched fist, makes up a small percentage of the deer's head volume. The rest of the deer's head may not be essential to maintain life from moment to moment, but without a nose, mouth and teeth in good working order there can be no long-term survival.

Obviously, most head shots are taken during the firearms season. I have encountered a number of cases where a jaw

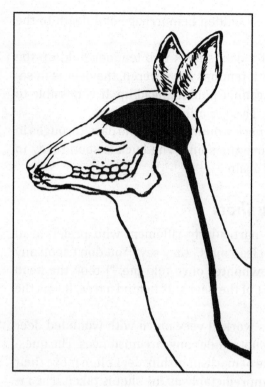

The brain of a deer is the size of a man's fist and makes up only a quarter of a deer's head.

injury occurred when there was no intention of making a head shot. At the last moment the deer dropped its head and caught the bullet in the wrong place.

Signs of a Jaw Injury

Injuries to the head are easy to identify once you know what to look for. You may see the deer's unsupported jaw hanging down. At the hit site there are likely to be small fragments of bone and teeth. This is one of the reasons why it is so important to go back to the original point of impact when you begin to track.

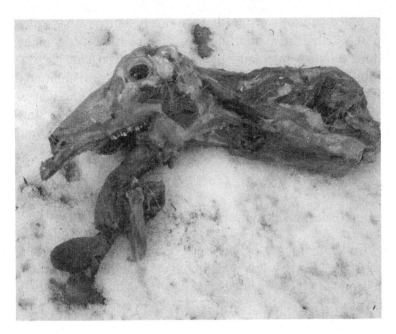

Only a deer's jaw was broken by the shotgun slug. This deer would have lived for more than a week if it had not been tracked and killed.

Generally, there is insufficient bleeding to permit easy eye-tracking after the first few hundred yards. But a deer with a mouth wound will, from time to time, shake its head in pain as it travels. This produces ropey strands of saliva tinged with blood that are shaken out at a 90 degree angle to the trail. At the deer's bed, blood and saliva will lie outside of the indentation formed by the body of the bedded deer.

Methods of Tracking and Taking a Jaw-Shot Deer

A jaw-shot deer is doomed, but catching up to it is very difficult unless the deer is a fawn. In places such as big swamps with heavy cover, it may be impossible.

Once you are certain that you are dealing with an ultimately lethal head shot, do not attempt to track at night. Move the deer into some dense holding cover and "park" it until daylight. When you have good long-range visibility try to push the deer into open hard woods or fields and hedgerows, where a careful, long range shot is possible on a slow moving deer. In many cases the hanging lower jaw is a certain means of identifying the right deer.

Summary

- Don't take head and neck shots intentionally.

- Broken-jaw shots, deliberate or accidental, are always killers in the long run. It is difficult to get close to a deer with an injured jaw. Track during daylight when distance visibility is good.

Chapter 7

AFTER THE SHOT
TO WAIT OR NOT TO WAIT

"Wait for the deer to lie down and stiffen up" is a piece of traditional after-the-shot advice that goes back at least 150 years. When modern bowhunting began, bowhunters accepted this waiting strategy and advocated waiting at least a half hour after the shot before following any wounded deer. **In many cases this was bad advice**, but the idea persists that you will lose your deer if you push it too soon. The majority of deer hunting books still repeat this. In the 80s the idea was successfully challenged in *Deer and Deer Hunting* articles by Rob Wegner and Al Hofacker, but the stiffening up theory dies hard. Most deer hunters I talk with still believe in it. Of course they may set aside this rule when weather, numerous hunters or the threat of coyotes make waiting for the deer to stiffen up an impractical strategy.

The question of how long to wait after the shot before you begin tracking is not a simple one. Throughout this book it has been stressed that it is a mistake to dump all wounded deer cases into the same bag and handle them all in the same way. In the last two chapters I've touched several times upon the waiting issue as it's related to various types of wounds inside and outside the body cavity. All wounded deer situations cannot be approached in the same way.

Since the strategies of how soon to track are so important, so confusing and so controversial, it seems worthwhile to review it all in this special chapter. I'll do my best to present what I have learned from tracking so many deer and also reading everything I could find on the subject.

The prevailing theory has long been that "if you don't spook a deer after the shot, it will usually go less than 200 yards before it beds down. If undisturbed, it will either die or stiffen up to the point that it can't move. Then it can be dispatched easily by the hunter with the wisdom to wait." The old authorities have not always agreed upon the best length for the waiting period.

The "stiffening up theory" has no evidence to support it, but it has an established place in the traditional lore of hunting. Personally I have jumped 100s of deer from their wound beds at least four hours after they had been wounded. Often I observed weakness, but I never saw any evidence of stiffness. A surge of adrenaline would give these frightened and weakened deer a burst of energy as they took off. The stiffness that hunters observe in dead deer is called *rigor mortis*, and it sets in only after death.

There are many good reasons why the hunter will usually do best by tracking slowly and carefully after the shot, and **after he has identified the nature of the deer's wound**.

Initial Shock Factor

The initial shock factor is seldom considered by the hunters of the "always wait" school. Shock sets in within minutes after a traumatic injury. We know a great deal about this from military combat medicine. The wounded soldier feels drowsy and disoriented. The medics will order him to lie down and stay calm because they know that this will increase chances of survival. I have had the privilege to interview two soldiers who took a bullet through a lung in World War II. They both survived due to prompt medical treatment. Their recollection was that after being shot they felt weak and drowsy, but they felt no pain. Pain came later when the shock wore off, and then it was alleviated somewhat with morphine.

If we transfer these experiences to the wounded deer case, we can see that the period of initial shock is a time when a deer's survival instincts are muddled. The shock factor is greater when a heavy bullet or slug is involved, but shock can also result from rapid and heavy blood loss, internal or external, that is produced by a broadhead. This is a time to approach carefully for a finishing shot rather than wait in your stand and hope for the best. And when we consider the "let'em lie down and stiffen up" theory we realize that it does not make much sense to let the deer do what the combat medics *recommend for survival.*

Chest Shots and Loss of Blood

When the deer is not brought down quickly by a heart or double lung shot, it is usually loss of blood volume that produces irreversible shock and death. A deer kept on the move loses more blood and produces a better blood trail. Scientific research has shown that the heart rate of a running deer is three times greater than its heart rate when bedded. Your own heart does something similar when you get out of your arm chair and go out for a jog. It's not a big stretch to conclude that a moving deer is going to be easier to track. The wound will keep bleeding because the increased blood pressure and flow will flush out blood clots as they form at the wound. Internal bleeding from the lungs will be greater if the blood circulation is accelerated.

Hofacker's research, based on over 1100 hunters' reports, indicates that wounded deer usually don't bed in the first 200 yards. If they die, they are more likely to collapse in stride as they try to get away. Hofacker's conclusions are in line with my own observations. In my own tracking experience I have found that deer are much more likely to stand and drip than to actually bed down in the early stages of a track.

Leg and Shoulder Hits

As already discussed in Chapter 4, leg and shoulder-hit deer will seldom bleed to death unless pushed. Normally they will go a few hundred yards and then stand and drip. The deer will be reluctant to bed because it is painful to get up and down. It will also feel more able to escape from danger if it stays on its feet. The hunter's waiting period gives the resting deer time to stop bleeding and to clot up. When the hunter does track up to the deer in an hour or so, the deer will usually move out at the sounds of his approach. The hunter will find a circle of blood drops where the deer stood, but no deer. Eye-tracking from this point without blood will be a slow task. Unless there is a tracking snow to speed his progress, the hunter will likely fail to get the deer bleeding again.

An Exception: Shots to the Stomach, Liver and Intestines

The wait strategy does make sense in the case of hits to the stomach, liver and intestines. Often these wounds don't bleed very much on the outside, even if the deer is pushed. The deer is more likely to lie down than when the running gear is damaged; in any case bleeding is likely to be intermittent after the first few hundred yards. The stomach often rotates so that the opening in the stomach is not aligned with the opening in the deer's side; bleeding from the inside of the stomach is shut off from the outside. On gut shots, a fold of intestine may block the external wound. After such wounds stop bleeding on the outside, you have to hope that the deer will stay in the area where you found the last blood or a bed. There is possibility that you can continue on the trail using the eye-tracking techniques discussed in the next chapter. But sometimes these deer can go a long way. I have tracked many stomach, gut or liver-shot deer that had gone over a mile without being pushed. They left little or no blood for an eye-tracker. Even if you are an expert eye-tracker, who can work a line without blood, it will take you a long time to follow for this distance on bare ground. And the coyotes do not wait. If a tracking dog is available, this may be your best solution.

Gut-shot deer are among the easiest for a dog to track. Deer shot in the large intestine are trackable with a dog, but here the problem is that they may stay alive for many days.

The coyotes don't wait until tomorrow morning.

Deciding on the appropriate waiting periods after the shot is one of the toughest judgment calls in deer hunting. So many things have to be considered:

1. Is it so warm that the venison will spoil if not found within eight hours?
2. Is there a tracking snow?
3. Is there a threat that rain or snow will erase your blood trail?
4. Is there a danger that another hunter will find your deer?
5. Are coyotes numerous?
6. Is there a danger that your deer, if pushed, will go onto a property where you cannot follow?
7. Finally, and very important, is the deer wounded in such a way that pushing it gently will improve the blood trail and the likelihood that the deer will hemorrhage to death?

One thing is certain. **Unless you can actually see the deer from your stand, you should go cautiously, but promptly, to the hit site. Check everything. Then you will be ready to decide when and how to proceed.**

Summary

• Unless you can see the deer, go cautiously to the hit site after the shot.

• Evaluation of sign at the hit site is essential before you begin tracking.

• Your tactics depend on the nature of the wound and the seven factors listed.

Chapter 8

BLOOD TRACKING

I have great respect for the skilled eye-tracker! Many times I have been asked to bring my tracking dog to help out a hunter when he finally ran out of any trail that he could track by eye. As I went over the first part of the line again with my tracking dog, I could not help but be impressed as I saw what this hunter had accomplished. In addition to droplets of blood, many other clues had been used to advance the line a half mile or more. In the North, where I have done my own tracking with a dog, eye-tracking is respected as an art, and recognized as a basic part of bowhunting. This tradition comes out of our pioneer hunting tradition, and the legacy left to us by American Indian bowhunters.

In Deer Search, a tracking dog organization in New York State, we have always presented our tracking dog service as **an agency of last resort**. Our policy in New York is this: When all eye-tracking efforts fail, then, and only then, should you resort to the tracking dog.

In other parts of the USA traditions are quite different. In many areas of Texas the standard advice to hunters is: "Don't try to track more than a 100 yards by yourself. You are likely to mess up the track, and make it much more difficult for a tracking dog later on. You are likely to push the deer so it goes much farther." The hot, dry Texas clay makes tracking difficult for man and dog alike. In Texas this advice makes good sense. In the South you will hear variations of the same theme. Scenting conditions are better than in most parts of the Southwest, but the vegetation can be incredibly dense. For the eye-tracker a dead deer can be very difficult to find, even if it is only a few feet away. In that country you don't want to follow your tracking dog for miles. You hope that you will jump a wounded deer after a short distance. Often the dog then runs the deer down and bays him off lead.

In guided hunts, outfitters are unenthusiastic about having bowhunters tracking through the woods while other clients are still bowhunting. Their forceful advice to clients is, "Don't follow if you hit a deer and it goes out of sight. We will find the deer for you after the hunt is over."

But no matter where you live, eye-tracking is important. In most parts of the country it is your primary approach to finding the deer. Even if you use a tracking dog, reading sign by eye is the best way to learn where the deer was hit. When you have an inexperienced tracking dog, it is a way of being sure that the dog is on the right line.

Knowing how to read "sign" for yourself can be essential for determining the appropriate waiting time before tracking. You can avoid pushing a deer that should be left to bed down and die close by. On the other hand, you can save yourself the effort of tracking fruitlessly when the available sign clearly shows that the deer was superficially wounded.

Tracking Suggestions

One common mistake is to ignore the very first part of the track where in many cases you will see the most evidence that can help you. Another mistake is to look only on the ground for blood sign. We have discussed the sign of various types of hits already. You are most likely to see these indications at the hit site. All too often hunters take right off in the direction they saw the deer headed. These hunters may miss a lot of very useful information. **It is essential to know what you are dealing with as you make your decision to track right away, to wait a half hour or to wait eight hours!**

Your first step is to mark the point where you were standing or sitting when you shot. Highly visible biodegradable tape is best. Then using this first marker as a reference point, move carefully to the hit site. Mark this also with the tape hung at eye level. The hit site marker will be an important point of reference when you actually start tracking.

Inspecting the Hit Site

Before moving out to track, make sure that you have searched the hit site area thoroughly for any hair, blood or other sign. When the deer has been shot with a firearm, hair, bone fragments and tissue may be spread out from the exit wound for up to ten yards. Experiments with rifle shots through a suspended dead deer show that blood and other sign are blown out in a cone from the exit wound and are projected well beyond where the deer was standing. It is easy to miss these important clues.

Sometimes it does happen that there is no sign at all except for scuff marks right at the hit site. You may not find blood sign for 50 yards or even 200 yards. Flagging the hit site will be useful as you search out ahead for the sign made by the deer you shot.

Looking for Sign....on the Ground and Above it!

Blood tracking is often presented in hunter training courses as a process of spotting blood on the ground. If you look only

Photo taken at an ACCSQ Blood Tracking Workshop in Quebec. In this experiment rifle bullets were shot through a suspended road kill. Blood and fragments, indicating the actual shot trajectory through the deer, were blown out on to the sheet behind.

on the ground, you will miss blood smears on weeds and saplings that show how high the deer was wounded. If the blood smears are 28 inches off the ground, this is not a good sign. In all likelihood the deer was hit too high to be recoverable. You should hope to see smears extending from 20 to 24 inches downward, depending on the size of the deer.

Remember that in deer hunting you should never draw final conclusions on the basis of one piece of evidence.

Often a stomach or gut-shot deer will leave bright red blood drops and smears. These come from the surface flesh of the deer, not from the internal organs. If you see a single trace of dark, muddy blood, or one fragment of stomach content, the importance of this outweighs all the bright red sign that you have observed. You have a gut-shot deer for sure, and you are highly likely to find it if you do not push and jump it too soon.

As you begin tracking a blood trail, you know, of course, its direction. After a few hundred yards, however, it can become vitally important to determine direction from the shape of the blood drops and smears. It very often happens that a decent blood line abruptly stops. What happened?

In many cases the line ends because the deer retraced its steps. Perhaps it was spooked by something up ahead. It's possible that it changed its mind about where to go. Anyway, whitetails do backtrack a lot, and you have to determine whether this is a possibility in your case.

There are situations in which a deer mills around in circles. Often this is in a big briar patch or swamp. It is easier to find the exit to this maze if you can determine the deer's direction of travel around the loops of blood trail.

Establishing the direction of travel is not complicated. As each blood drop falls from a moving deer, the ground spatters, or "fingers" point in the direction of travel. Not every drop will show clear pointing fingers. You will have to search until you find several pointing in the same direction.

If you suspect a backtrack when a blood trail dead-ends, check for blood splatters pointing both ways on the trail. This will tell you whether you should range out beyond the apparent dead end looking for more blood, or whether the best tactic is to work backward on the blood trail, looking for the point where the deer broke off in a new direction.

It is important to mark the trail as you go. My own preferred marking is a roll of blaze orange, biodegradable tape. Tie it to branches or weeds at eye level so that it will be easy to return to the last drop or smear. Toilet paper on the ground can also be used, although it is a little harder to find again later. Once you have a line of markers up (or down on the ground), you will recognize the general direction of the deer's travel. It will be easier to look in likely places for the next blood droplet.

Tracking, putting up markers and watching ahead for the deer, all at the same time, is really too much for one person to do. A tracking team of two is much better. One tracks and marks. The other tracks a bit and mainly watches ahead, ready for a shot if the opportunity comes.

When Blood Tracking Gets Tough

If the blood trail dwindles down to occasional drops, you will have to use your good judgment to know where to look for the next one. When a deer is wounded it will usually travel the same routes that it frequented when healthy. Younger deer will follow established deer runs. Older deer, especially wise old bucks, will move through the thickest funnels and hedgerows, just as they ordinarily do.

If you track to the edge of a pasture or a mowed hay field, there are alternatives to spending hours looking for blood drops that have fallen down between the blades of grass. If there is a fence around the open pasture, it is more efficient to work the perimeter checking the gaps where deer have been squeezing under or between the fence wires. As the wounded deer crouches down to pass under the wire, it is very likely to bleed a few drops onto the ground. If you know where to look, you will find this sign. Deer trails exiting out of an unfenced field are another place to look. These are not as productive as fence gaps, but it is still much easier to see blood on a deer run than in a grassy field.

A wounded deer will pick a gap in a barbed wire fence line to escape across afield. Look for blood and possibly hair here.

In the Northeast there are many stone walls built by early farmers. Trees later reclaimed these early fields, but the tumble down walls are still there. You will find low spots in these walls that deer choose as crossing points. When the deer stretches a bit to cross there will generally be a drop or two on the stones. Checking at these likely spots may help you bridge a 200-yard interval where you could find no blood at all.

Wounded deer will pick a low spot in a stone wall to cross. Look for blood on rocks where they stretch to get over.

Trails on steep banks and hill sides are another place to look for blood. The exertion and stretching involved with going up and down hill, is likely to produce a few drops of blood that will keep you going.

By the way, there is absolutely nothing to this bit of folklore about wounded deer not going uphill. They do it all the time. Many times I have found deer dead at the top of a knoll or ridge. Climbing that hill was the last thing they did before they died. They went to that spot, just as they did in ordinary times, because it gave them visibility in the directions where they could not smell danger. They knew that with one jump they could be out of sight if danger approached from any direction.

When you are stalled on a difficult track, check the high spots where many hunters do not bother to look.

Deer wounded in the stomach or small intestines are very likely to go to water and die there. This is not true for deer wounded elsewhere in the body.

Tracking at Night

Many deer are shot as dusk approaches, and they begin to move out and feed. If a deer happens to be wounded at this time, late in the day, it often means that tracking it must be done in the dark. To track at night you will need a good light. Law Enforcement generally frowns upon the use of large, high candlepower lights suitable for jacking deer, but you will probably need more of a light than you have carried with you all day as you hunted. Mark your point of loss well as you return to your truck to get assistance and appropriate lighting equipment.

What is a suitable light? You need a flashlight that will last for several hours.

Forget pen lights. At the present time (2010), the LED lights available to hunters do not give enough illumination to track well and also check for a deer out ahead of you. The high-intensity lithium battery powered Xenon flashlights have the disadvantage of burning out too rapidly. You may be several hours in the woods, so if you use them, carry extra batteries. At present, personally, I still prefer a standard light with six alkaline D-Cell batteries.

You need a flashlight in the 200 Lumen class for night tracking. LED applications in flashlights are being improved rapidly, and useful flashlights are declining rapidly in price.

Gasoline lanterns that produce an intense white light will make fresh red blood show up clearly; Coleman is a manufacturer of these, and they are definitely an asset although a bit awkward to carry. Do not use them if a tracking dog is going to be involved in the search. The fumes from the light interfere with the dog's effectiveness.

The "Gerber Carnivore Blood Light" flashlight has been much advertised as assistance for seeing blood when tracking at night. It has a combination of red and blue LEDs that are supposed to make blood stand out clearly. I have carried a "Carnivore" on my tracking calls with my dog, and I found it to be no improvement over a regular flashlight. At my suggestion hunters have borrowed my own Carnivore to back me up in spotting for blood. I have never encountered anyone who found the Gerber Carnivore to be of practical use. The color blind hunters that tested my light did not find it particularly helpful.

Color and Color Blindness

Red, drop-like spots are seen on fallen red maple leaves early in the season. They can make tracking difficult even for the hunter with normal color vision. The sure test here is to wet the spot with saliva. If it smudges, it's probably blood. If the spot stays as before, the color is part of the leaf itself.

A chemical product called BlueStar detects a blood component called hemoglobin and makes it glow in low-light conditions. It was originally developed to help Law Enforcement personnel detect traces of human blood. If you have a color vision problem, suspicious brown spots can be sprayed to see if they are actually blood. BlueStar will foam and glow on hemoglobin, even if rain has made the blood invisible to the eye.

You can't spray a swath of BlueStar for half a mile as you follow your buck. That would be a bit expensive. However, for checking out a specific place, such as a fence or stone wall, it can be useful. This product actually does what the manufacturer claims.

An inability to distinguish red from dark brown is a problem with which a surprising number of deer hunters have to deal. This disability, which is genetically based, can make life especially difficult for the bowhunter. He needs good hunting buddies to help him. And he should not overlook the natural skills of a non-hunting wife or girlfriend. Color blindness is much rarer in women than in men. It seems to go beyond this. Many times my tracking associates and I have been in the woods on deer calls with women who have had no experience tracking wounded deer. Yet their eyes picked up tiny droplets of red blood that the more experienced males missed. Perhaps this is a matter of genetics, but it could also be that many women are more accustomed to making subtle color distinctions than do men.

It is worthwhile for a color blind hunter to carry a one ounce container of hydrogen peroxide with him. A suspicious spot on a leaf can be tested. If it foams it may be blood...or squirrel poop. The peroxide reacts with both substances, but the squirrel poop will have a more solid consistency than blood. Peroxide can be helpful for the color blind hunter.

Deer Finding Gadgets

Handheld infrared heat detectors have been on the market for some time. If you like a gadget for every circumstance, you might choose to buy one. Most of the deer I have tracked went too far to be located by an infrared heat sensor, but in the right circumstances, with a deer that doesn't go far, they might be useful. If I didn't have a tracking dog, I would use one to find a deer in a five-year-old clearcut, grown up in briars.

The string tracker is a gadget manufactured by Gametracker that has been used for many years by a few bowhunters. A light, 22 pound test line is attached to the arrow at the broadhead. When the arrow is shot into a deer, the attached line peels off a spool, mounted on the bow, and theoretically guides the hunter to his deer.

The string tracker is used most in bear hunting over bait. The shooting range is short so the string influences the arrow trajectory very little. At the shot, the bear dives off into the dense cover taking the tracking string along with him. Even if he only goes a hundred yards, he can be very difficult to find without the string tracker.

A bow with the string tracker mounted must be maneuvered with great care before the shot, because the loose string extending from the bow to the arrowhead is prone to hanging up at the most inopportune moment. Another problem with the string tracker is that the extended string almost always breaks if the deer or bear goes very far. It does give a direction of passage, and that can be of help.

A handheld GPS can help you in tracking or searching if you are thoroughly comfortable with it and don't let the technology distract you from close observation. It will give you the big picture of where you have already tracked and what destination the deer had in mind.

If it comes down to a situation in which you can't find your deer through your own best efforts and tracking skills, then it is unlikely that any of the items discussed above are going to save the day. They are more likely to make the task of finding a deer a bit easier.

The one "gadget" most likely to find your deer, when all else fails, is a trained, experienced tracking dog. You don't have to own one, but you need to know where you can call for the dog and handler to help you out.

Summary

• Mark the trail you are following with biodegradable tape or toilet paper.

• When tracking becomes difficult, gaps in wire fences or stone walls are good places to look for blood.

• Search for blood on deer trails exiting a field when you can't track your way across.

• Wounded deer readily go up hill, if they have a reason to do so.

• Gut-shot deer DO go to water.

Chapter 9

WHEN THE BLOOD TRAIL ENDS

In this book it has been stressed that the *amount* of blood found on the trail of a wounded deer is not a reliable indication of what has happened inside that deer. Mortally wounded deer often lose little blood externally. Sometimes the deer does not leave enough blood trail to make tracking it by eye a possibility. Other means must be found.

In so-called "blood tracking" with dogs, the dog is actually tracking without blood much of the time. The dog uses the individual scent of the deer and microscopic scent particles coming down from the wound in order to follow it.

Good tracking dogs are not always accessible, and in many cases the hunter will prefer finding the deer entirely by his own efforts. He understands that tracking wounded deer can involve much more than finding drops or smears of blood. He is aware that tracking footprints is a slow process that may allow scavengers, such as coyotes, to steal his venison. He is ready to take the risk.

In the real world of eye-tracking, blood sign and other indications of passage are mingled together. Probably you will begin by using scuffed leaves and hoof prints as a means of getting you from one blood trace to another one a hundred yards away, There are even times when a mortally wounded deer will not leak any blood at all externally.

A deer, weakened by a wound will often drag his feet leaving disturbances in the dry leaves of the forest floor. You will be able to see these better if you lie down flat and look ahead parallel to the ground. These scuff marks also show up better when the sun is close to the horizon at the beginning and the end of the day.

Following hoof prints can be very difficult because there are usually so many other deer tracks in the area. A tracking stick will help in this situation.

length of front hoof

width of front hoof

stride length of deer

Cut yourself a small, green branch of finger thickness and about two feet long. Then find a footprint that you are sure is from your deer. At one end of your tracking stick, use your knife to mark out the length and width of the foot print. Since the front hoofs are slightly longer and wider than the rear ones, you should mark the dimensions of both the larger and the smaller prints. When you are far enough from the hit site to be sure that the deer was walking, determine the length of a walking stride. Mark that distance on your stick with a strong, deep notch at the appropriate distance from the other, unmarked end of the tracking

Tracking stick

stick. With your tracking stick you will be able to determine exactly where to look for the next print as you work forward. After the first 100 yards or so, you may not need the tracking stick any more.

The scuff and footprint approach requires discipline and practice. It will not appeal to everyone, and its effectiveness is dependent on the surface involved. Frozen ground makes observing ground disturbance much more difficult. Rain can erase the subtle signs you need to see. Snow can conceal them.

The experienced tracker's eye can read foot sign with remarkable speed independent of a tracking stick. With sufficient time and application you would be able to learn to read an individual deer's path as effectively. Your own eyes have learned to swiftly scan all the tiny symbols on this page, but of course this required years of education and practice. The problem is that few of us today have the time to develop this level of eye-tracking skill. African trackers have maintained this art, which has been lost in most parts of the modern world.

If you wish to explore the world of eye-tracking more deeply, begin with the book entitled Tom Brown's *Field Guide to Nature Observation and Tracking*. Tom Brown did not write this book for hunters, but it contains an abundance of information that hunters can use.

Where Deer Bed Down

Wounded deer generally have a secure place in mind, and often they will try to return to it to bed down. Surprisingly, they will pass through what looks like good bedding cover, and then leave it to cross open fields in order to get to their own special place. This may be close by, and in this case a buck or a doe may make a large circle while staying in the same general area. If a buck in rut is out of its home territory looking for does, it will start for home and travel as far as it can in that direction. A GPS can help you determine where it is headed.

Wounded deer will often bed and die in overgrown fields because they know that hunters are more likely to stay and move around in big timber. The dense grass and weeds are their safe bedding area, where they go while hunters are driving the obvious spots and complaining about the lack of deer.

Often a stomach-shot deer will try to go to a waterhole, pond or creek because it is dehydrated and very thirsty. There it dies in the water or on the bank. Always check water in the area.

In a creek or river, the deer carcass may float down stream a considerable distance before it hangs up in a fallen tree or a shallow spot. Walk the banks checking carefully for that grey-brown bulge. Wind and current can carry the carcass quite a distance. Fortunately cold water preserves the quality of the venison for a long time.

Aside from this special case, wounded deer generally refuse to bed down in water. They do like to bed on a small hummock or island in a swamp, but actually lying in water is not an option for them unless they know that they are being pursued and are trying to hide.

The final bedding place is not predictable unless you are very familiar with the area. Weakness may suddenly overtake the deer, and it may even collapse in the middle of an open field. A characteristic last move is to "J" around and bed down in a position to observe the back trail. They die in that spot.

Crows and Ravens

When searching for lost deer be aware of the many clues that nature offers. Crows, almost everywhere, and ravens in the North are excellent indicators. Watch for crows clustered in trees along the skyline. They may be watching and waiting for a meal to develop. They will call for others to assemble with them, but they are not strong enough to consume very much until some larger predator, such as a coyote, breaks into the deer and eats its fill. Crow efforts will be restricted to pecking into the eyes and at the wound once the deer is dead. Their specialty is cleaning up what the coyotes leave behind.

Don't be distracted from your tracking or searching activity by every crow commotion that you hear. Crows enjoy harassing the great horned owls that prey upon them at night. A storm of loud cawing and wheeling about in the air usually means that they have found an owl, not a deer.

Ravens are the best indictor of a wounded or dead deer. These northern birds, larger than a crow, with coarser bills, have an effective working relationship with coyotes. The ravens make aerial surveys and announce their finds with croaking calls as they perch in trees around the dead or dying deer. The coyotes understand the meaning of these raven croaks and come running. After the coyotes have opened up the deer and eaten their fill they withdraw, and the ravens enjoy their reward. You must beat the coyotes to your deer.

Grid Searches

A disciplined and persevering grid search will produce the dead deer in some kinds of cover, such as an overgrown field, a vast thicket or an un-harvested corn field. Adjust your tactics to the vegetation and terrain. Each traverse taken by you and your hunting buddies should be parallel to the next and close enough so that there is no possibility of walking past the deer. This can mean that in some dense cover you must search strips as little as six feet apart. Use strips of marking tape hung high so that you can maintain straight, parallel traverses. A GPS can help you here!

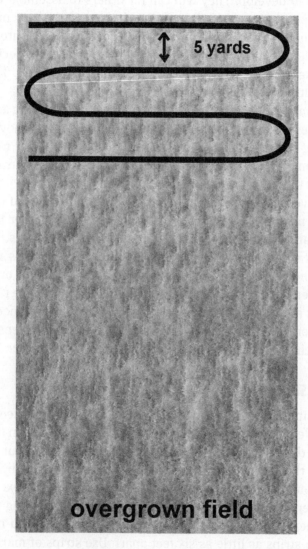

5 yards

overgrown field

Grid search pattern

Viewed from one side, the white belly of a deer shows up very well. Check out anything white. It may be a rock, a sun-bleached log or the deer. If the deer is lying down with his legs extended away from you, all you will see is the brown back that blends with the ground cover. A deer's back is much more difficult to notice.

In more open areas if you are searching along lines 50 feet apart, it is quite possible to walk past a doe or small antlered buck lying on its side in knee-high grass. Deer are narrow, and they lie very flat.

Grid searches are monotonous work. It is easier to justify the time spent if you do it thoroughly so that you can say afterward, "I'm sure my deer isn't there."

Summary

• Eye-tracking is a learned skill not limited to finding drops of blood.

• Eye-tracking works best when the sun is close to the horizon and your eyes are low, looking out along the surface of the ground.

• Don't assume that the deer will stop in the first good bedding cover.

• Check all sources of water in the case of gut-shot deer.

• Watch for crows and ravens.

• Grid searches are effective in un-mowed fields and dense, brushy areas.

The Passion of the Hunt

Those who hunt know that hunting is different from civilized daily life. When we hunt, or when we look for a lost deer, we do not justify this in terms of some cost/benefit analysis: "What are the horns, hide and venison worth? What is our time worth?" Hunting and searching is driven by passion and then conducted by our best reason and intuition. Our hunting passion coincides with our hunting ethics.

Sometimes there is an overpopulation of deer, but this is no excuse for sloppy hunting. The ethical hunter does everything he can to kill cleanly and not lose a deer. He searches hard for every deer he shoots. He does not think simply in terms of statistics or what is biologically significant. He has a personal, one-on-one relationship with that particular deer, and he has a sense of responsibility for it.

When we hunt or search for a wounded deer, our feelings are complex. There is something of the predator in our feelings. We become a part of the natural world, "wild" humans seeking to take our prey before some wilder coyote finds it and devours it.

At the same time we have another desire to do what is "right" although we know that this ethical sense comes from our civilized background and not from the natural world. We are aware that the natural world is cruel, that the lives of wild animals are destined to end through violence, disease or starvation. This does not change our conviction that we should do everything we can to reduce suffering and prevent waste. As hunters, and as trackers, we are predators, but we can be more humane predators than wolves and coyotes. We are predators ethically responsible for how we treat our prey. As hunters we are on the edge between the natural and the civilized worlds.

About the Author

John Jeanneney is a retired university professor whose heart has always been in the woods. As a hunter, who had lost deer himself, John became obsessed with finding better way to prevent this kind of losses from happening. His widely selling book *Tracking Dogs for Finding Wounded Deer* was one outcome of this. It received strong reviews from around the world. Readers pointed out that this book has much new information about wounded deer for all hunters, even if they had no access to a tracking dog. *Dead On!* expands on the deer part of his earlier Tracking Dogs book.

John loves to write and to share what he has learned with fellow hunters. Numerous articles, teaching workshops, and long hours of tracking during deer season have helped him deal with the pains of "retirement".

For more information about John and his writing go to his websites at:

www.deadonbook.com

www.born-to-track.com

Also by John Jeanneney

Tracking Dogs for Finding Wounded Deer

Autor is available online

www.deadonbook.com

www.born-to-track.com

Version 1.0 June 2010

CPSIA information can be obtained
at www.ICGtesting.com
Printed in the USA
BVOW06s1328010317
477466BV00009B/204/P